Joy to the World

Lynda Milligan & Nancy Smith

D0791480

POSSIBILITIES®

...Publishers of DreamSpinners® patterns, I'll Teach Myself® sewing products, and Possibilities® books...

Acknowledgements

We would like to dedicate this book to our longtime friend and first employee, Ruth Haggbloom. Ruth walked into our store, Great American Quilt Factory, in 1984, shortly after we opened. She was walking her dog and stopped in to see what we had. She volunteered to open the store if we were unable to get in because of bad weather. We hired her and also got her husband, Orrie, as a bonus. Little did Ruth know that eighteen years later she would still be a part of Great American Quilt Factory. Thank you, Ruth, for all your support and friendship.

Thanks again to Blue Rabbit Ltd. gift shop for allowing us to photograph in their store. Blue Rabbit's phone number is 303-843-9419. Thanks also to Aina Martin for letting us photograph in her beautiful home.

With love from Lynda and Nancy.

Our Stitchers & Quilters

A special thanks to all our friends who made a block for the Christmas Houses quilt. Each block is delightful and so creative. All your names appear on the chart at the bottom of page four. Also, thanks to Joanne Malone, Jan Hagan, Jane Dumler, Karen McCarter, Carolyn Schmitt, Sandi Fruehling, Ann Petersen, and Sharon Holmes for their stitching and quilting expertise.

Together we write great books
of which we can all be proud.

Credits

Sharon Holmes — Editing, Production Art
Debbe Linn — Cover, Photo Styling, Production Art
Sara Tuttle — Hand Illustration, Pattern Design
Valerie Perrone — Design
Chris Scott — Copy Reading
Sandi Fruehling — Copy Reading
Brian Birlauf — Photography
Lee Milne — Digital Photography, Cover Photo

POSSIBILITIES®
…Publishers of DreamSpinners® patterns, I'll Teach
Myself® sewing products, and Possibilities® books…

Joy to the World

© 1999 Lynda Milligan & Nancy Smith

All rights reserved. No part of this book may be reproduced in any form without permission of the authors, with one exception: Permission is granted to photocopy and enlarge patterns for individual use. The written instructions, photographs, and designs are intended for the retail purchaser and are under federal copyright laws. Projects may not be manufactured for commercial sale.

Published in the United States of America by Possibilities®, Denver, Colorado.

Library of Congress Catalog Card Number: 99-070357
ISBN: 1-880972-38-7

Photo Index

We try to fill our books with as many projects as possible. Because of this, some patterns in this book will need to be enlarged on a copier or with a home computer/scanner setup. We know this may be an inconvenience, but we are sure you will be delighted with your finished project. Our favorite method of applique for these projects is the fusible web technique with a buttonhole stitch finish. Patterns are reversed and ready to be traced. Be sure to have plenty of fusible web on hand if using this method. Add seam allowance to patterns if doing hand applique.

This great Christmas Houses quilt was made by some of our employees during November, *before* the Christmas crunch.

Everyone was given five pattern pieces—house, porch or shed, window, door, and chimney. The block was to be returned to us trimmed to 14½″ including seam allowance. Participants could do their own machine buttonhole stitch or leave that last detailing for us to finish. Everyone used their own fabrics and their own ideas, as you can see! The house was made taller or shorter, the number of windows and chimneys was varied, and the shed was used or left out as the scene required.

The best thing about the quilt is the creative detail that makes each block so unique. Novelty fabrics provide wood and rock textures and make possible minute details such as candles in the windows, banners or wreaths on the doors, and cactus in the front yard. The backgrounds are made up of wonderful sky fabrics and snowy or grassy prints. The trees, sidewalks, and window treatments are all different from block to block. Beads were used for Christmas lights. Photo transfers were used for faces in house and car windows. Our blocks include a church, an adobe house, a birdhouse, a crèche, a gingerbread house, a log cabin, and several versions of warm, welcoming houses all decked out for Christmas.

We had great fun with this group quilt project and were in awe of all the creativity that was shown. Our only dilemma now is—we all want the quilt!

Be sure to make a chart on the back that includes the participants' names and the year the quilt was made. See the name chart at the right that went on our quilt. It could be hand-drawn on muslin with permanent markers, done on a computer and made into a fabric transfer on a photocopy machine, or even embroidered. Just cut it out and applique it to the back of the quilt for a permanent record of the people involved. You might also want to have participants write a line or two about their blocks and include that on the label.

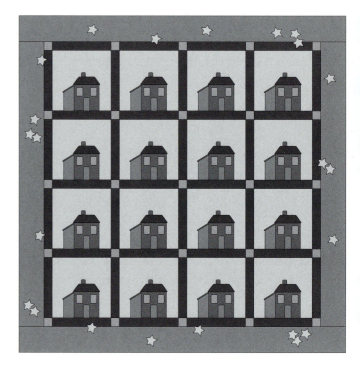

Christmas Houses – 1998

Sharon Holmes	Jean Denton	Joanne Malone	Susan Auskaps
Maggie Thomas	Debbe Linn	Lynda Milligan	Terri Wiley
Diana Leher	Nancy Smith	Judy Carpenter	Sara Tuttle
Denise Ramsburg	Valerie Perrone	Marie Gifford	Ann Petersen

·····Christmas Houses······

14″ block – 16 blocks set 4x4 with 2″ sashing

Photo on page 20

Approximate finished size 78x78″

Use 42-44″-wide fabric. When strips appear in the cutting list, cut crossgrain strips (selvage to selvage).

························Yardage························

Large scraps for sky & ground – up to 15″ squares
Medium & small scraps for appliques

Sashing rectangles	1⅝ yds.
Sashing squares	¼ yd.
Border	1¾ yds.
Backing	5 yds.
Binding	⅔ yd.
Batting	84x84″

························Cutting························

Sky & ground pieces	See Directions Step 1
Applique pieces	Patterns on page 79
Sashing	25 squares – 2½″
	40 rectangles – 2½x14½″
Border	8 strips 6½″ wide
Binding	8 strips 2½″ wide

························Directions························

Use ¼″ seam allowance unless otherwise noted.

1. Get friends to make 16 blocks using basic house patterns on page 79 and their own ideas for other applique embellishment. Sky/ground can be two rectangles sewn together or it can be made with applique pieces (hills, etc.) over-lapping on a sky square. Blocks should be 14½″ including seam allowance, to finish at 14″. When you have everyone's blocks, press them and then trim to 14½″ if necessary.

2. Make five sashing rows with rectangles and squares.

3. Make four block rows with blocks and sashing rectangles.

4. Stitch rows together. Press well.

5. Border: Measure length of quilt. Piece border strips to the measured length and stitch to sides of quilt. Repeat at top and bottom. Press.

6. If desired, applique stars overlapping borders as shown in whole-quilt diagram.

7. Piece backing to same size as batting. Use your favorite layering, quilting, and binding methods to finish quilt.

·······Santa Stockings·······

Photo on page 28   Finished length 20″

Yardage For one stocking

Stocking & lining	¾ yd.
Appliques – scraps	up to 4x11″ & 5x6″
Binding	⅓ yd.
Batting – thin cotton	one piece 14x22″

Cutting Pattern on page 62

Stocking & lining	2 stockings, 2 reversed
Applique pieces	Patterns on pages 62, 71-76
Binding – bias	2½″ wide, pieced to 70″ long
Batting	one piece using pattern

Directions

1. Applique stocking front with your favorite method using photo and diagram as guides for placement. Lettering can be reduced on a copier for longer names.

2. Lay stocking front and lining wrong sides together with batting between. Baste ¼″ from outside edge. Quilt as desired. Lay stocking back and lining wrong sides together.

3. Press binding strip in half lengthwise, wrong sides together. Bind top edges of stocking front and back using a ⅜″ seam allowance.

4. Pin stocking front to stocking back, wrong sides together. Baste ¼″ from edge.

5. Bind raw edges with a ⅜″ seam allowance, leaving a 6″ tail at top left to make hanger and folding end to inside at top right.

6. For hanger, stitch folded edges of binding tail together. Fold raw end under on back of stocking and stitch in place.

Trees & Stars

Photos on pages 32 & 52

8″ block – 32 blocks set on point

Approximate finished size 58x69″

Use 42-44″-wide fabric. When strips appear in the cutting list, cut crossgrain strips (selvage to selvage).

Yardage

Background	3¾ yds.
Treetops – assorted greens	1 yd.
Tree trunks – brown	⅛ yd.
Stars – gold	⅝ yd.
Border 1	⅜ yd.
Border 2	1⅜ yds.
Backing	3⅞ yds.
Binding	⅝ yd.
Batting	64x75″

Cutting

NOTE: Use rotary cutting ruler with eighth-inch markings. To cut sixteenths, line up fabric between eighth-inch markings.

Background fabric

Star block	corners	56 squares – 3½″
	side units	56 rectangles – 2½x3½″
Tree block	center units	72 squares – 3⁵⁄₁₆″
	sides, tops	21 squares – 4⅞″ – cut in half diagonally
	trunk units	4 strips 3¼″ wide
Setting triangles	sides	4 squares – 12⅝″ – cut in **quarters** diagonally
	corners	2 squares – 6½″ – cut in half diagonally
Treetops	center units	36 rectangles 3⁵⁄₁₆x6³⁄₁₆″
	tops	6 squares – 4⅞″ – cut in half diagonally
Tree trunks		2 strips 1⅜″ wide
Stars	centers	14 squares – 2½″
	points	Pattern on page 76 56 & 56 reversed
Border 1		6 strips 1½″ wide
Border 2		7 strips 5½″ wide
Binding		7 strips 2½″ wide

Directions

Use ¼″ seam allowance unless otherwise noted.

1. Make 14 star blocks.

   a. Make side units. Match clipped points of triangle to raw edge of rectangle, right sides together. Stitch. Trim excess background to ¼″ seam allowance if desired. Press triangle over. Repeat on other side of rectangle. See diagram.

   b. Finish blocks as shown.

2. Make tree blocks:

   a. Make treetop sections as shown, using treetop rectangles and background squares (for center unit). Trim excess background to ¼″ seam allowance if desired. Stitch sections into 2-section trees and 3-section trees, as shown. Stitch background triangles to tops of 2-section trees and treetop fabric triangles to tops of 3-section trees (cut from the 4⅞″ squares).

b. Make strip sets with trunk and background strips. Cut into 6⅞″ segments. Cut segments into quarters diagonally. See diagram. Stitch trunk units to treetop sections.

c. Stitch background triangles to sides of blocks.

3. Stitch diagonal rows of blocks, side setting triangles, and corner setting triangles following diagrams. Refer to whole-quilt diagram for placement of 2- and 3-section trees.

4. Stitch rows together. Press well.

5. Border 1: Measure length of quilt. Piece border strips to the measured length and stitch to sides of quilt. Repeat at top and bottom. Press.

6. Border 2: Repeat Step 5. Press.

7. Piece backing horizontally to same size as batting. Use your favorite layering, quilting, and binding methods to finish quilt.

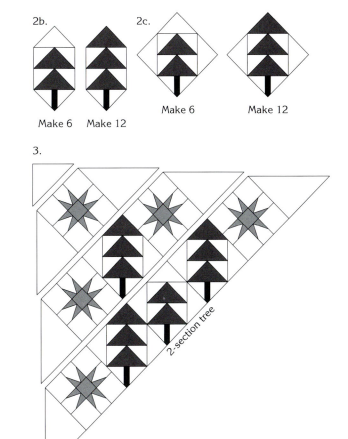

2b. 2c.

Make 6   Make 12   Make 6   Make 12

3.

2-section tree

1a-b.

Match clipped points   Trim   Make 56

Make 28   Make 14

Make 14

2a.   Make 36

Make 6   Make 12

2b.

Make 2

Holiday Gift Cakes
from Mildred Cap

8 oz. softened cream cheese
1 c. margarine
1½ c. sugar
1½ tsp. vanilla
4 eggs
2¼ c. sifted flour
1½ tsp. baking powder

¾ c. chopped maraschino cherries
½ c. very finely chopped nuts

Frosting
1½ c. sifted powdered sugar
2 tbsp. milk

Blend well the softened cream cheese, margarine, sugar, and vanilla. Add eggs one at a time, mixing well after each addition. Gradually add flour sifted with baking powder. Mix well. Fold in cherries. Grease 5 baby loaf pans (5x3x2″) and dust with very finely chopped nuts. Bake at 350° for 40-50 minutes. Remove from pans and cool on rack. Frost tops of loaves, letting frosting run down sides.

Special thanks to Denise Ramsburg
for sharing her mother's recipe.

Holly Berry
Log Cabin

Photo on page 64

16½″ block – 16 blocks set 4x4

Approximate finished size 66x66″

Use 42-44″-wide fabric. When strips appear in the cutting list, cut crossgrain strips (selvage to selvage).

Yardage

Lights
assorted whites to total	4 yds.

Darks
assorted reds & greens to total	4 yds.
Leaves to total	1½ yds.
Berries	⅛ yd.
Backing	4¼ yds.
Binding	⅝ yd.
Batting	72x72″

Cutting

Lights	Piece 1	16 squares – 2x2″
	Piece 2	16 rectangles – 2x3½″
	Piece 5	16 rectangles – 2x5″
	Piece 6	16 rectangles – 2x6½″
	Piece 9	16 rectangles – 2x8″
	Piece 10	16 rectangles – 2x9½″
	Piece 13	16 rectangles – 2x11″
	Piece 14	16 rectangles – 2x12½″
	Piece 17	16 rectangles – 2x14″
	Piece 18	16 rectangles – 2x15½″
Darks	Centers	16 squares – 2x2″
	Piece 3	16 rectangles – 2x3½″
	Piece 4	16 rectangles – 2x5″
	Piece 7	16 rectangles – 2x6½″
	Piece 8	16 rectangles – 2x8″
	Piece 11	16 rectangles – 2x9½″
	Piece 12	16 rectangles – 2x11″
	Piece 15	16 rectangles – 2x12½″
	Piece 16	16 rectangles – 2x14″
	Piece 19	16 rectangles – 2x15½″
	Piece 20	16 rectangles – 2x17″
Applique pieces		Patterns on page 65. 38 holly, 11 maple, & 8 oak leaves; 63 berries
Binding		7 strips 2½″ wide

Directions

Use ¼″ seam allowance unless otherwise noted.

1. Make 16 blocks in five counterclockwise rounds, placing fabrics randomly. See diagram. Press blocks.

2. Make four rows of four, rotating blocks as shown. Stitch rows together, rotating third and fourth rows 180° as shown in whole-quilt diagram. Press.

3. Applique leaves and berries on light sections using your favorite method.

4. Piece backing to same size as batting. Use your favorite layering, quilting, and binding methods to finish quilt.

1.

Round 1

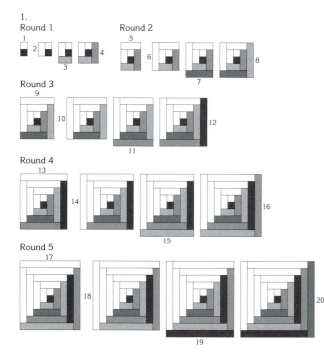

Round 2

Round 3

Round 4

Round 5

2. Make 2 of Each

·········Pull-a-Bow··········

Photo on page 61

These easy-to-make bows are reusable.

Finished sizes: 3″ and 4″ diameter

Use 42-44″-wide fabric.

Yardage

3″ diameter bow	⅛ yd. fabric – cotton, cotton lamé, silk, polyester, etc.
	1 yd. ¼″ ribbon
4″ diameter bow	¼ yd. fabric
	1½ yds. ¼″ ribbon

Cutting

Fabric for 3″ diameter bow	3x30″
Fabric for 4″ diameter bow	5x42-44″

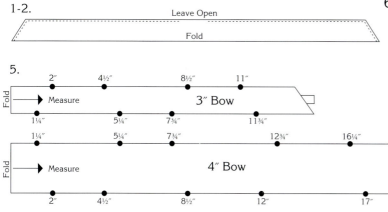

1-2.

Leave Open

Fold

5.

Fold

Measure

3″ Bow

2″ 4½″ 8½″ 11″

1¼″ 5¼″ 7¾″ 11¾″

Fold

Measure

4″ Bow

1¼″ 5¼″ 7¾″ 12¾″ 16¼″

2″ 4½″ 8½″ 12″ 17″

Directions

Use ¼″ seam allowance unless otherwise noted.

1. Fold strip lengthwise, right sides together. Cut 60° angles at each end. See diagram.

2. Stitch as shown, leaving a 2″ opening for turning at center of long side. Turn right side out. Press. Slipstitch opening closed.

3. Cut a piece of ribbon 1″ longer than the fabric piece. Fold fabric piece and ribbon in half crosswise and mark centers. Open out flat and lay ribbon on top of fabric piece. Tack the two together securely at center marks.

4. Refold, encasing ribbon inside. Make sure ribbon is centered so it won't get caught in stitching in next step.

5. Measure and mark for tacks from folded end as shown in diagram. Tack at each mark, making sure not to catch ribbon in stitching.

6. Pull on ribbon to form bow. Use ribbon ends to tie bow to basket handle, wine gift bag, or any other place that needs a pretty bow.

NOTE: These can be made with satin ribbon in place of the fabric piece. Two different colors of wide satin ribbon create a two-tone effect. Just place the two ribbons wrong sides together before tacking the pull ribbon to them.

Photo on page 53

10½″ block – 24 blocks set 4 x 6 with 1½″ sashing

Approximate finished size 67x91″

Use 42-44″-wide fabric. When strips appear in the cutting list, cut crossgrain strips (selvage to selvage).

Yardage

Darks – assorted reds	24 fat qtrs. or ¼ yd. pieces
Light (white)	6¼ yds.
Backing	5¾ yds.
Binding	¾ yd.
Batting	73 x 97″

Cutting

For one block (use one dark fabric)

Dark	claws	8 squares – 2⅜″ – cut in half diagonally
	paws	4 squares – 3½″
	center	1 square – 2″
Light	claw units	8 squares – 2⅜″ – cut in half diagonally
	sides	4 rectangles – 2 x 5″
	corners	4 squares – 2″
Sashing	light	35 squares – 2″
		58 rectangles – 2 x 11″
Border 1	light	8 strips 5¾″ wide
Border 2	mixed darks	96 squares – 2⅜″ – cut in half diagonally (4 of each)
	light	96 squares – 2⅜″ – cut in half diagonally
	light	4 squares – 2″
Border 3	light	9 strips 2½″ wide
Binding		9 strips 2½″ wide

Directions

Use ¼″ seam allowance unless otherwise noted.

1. Make 24 blocks following diagram. Press.

2. Make seven sashing rows with four sashing rectangles and five sashing squares.

3. Make six block rows with four blocks and five sashing rectangles.

4. Stitch rows together. Press well.

5. Border 1: Measure length of quilt. Piece border strips to the measured length and stitch to sides of quilt. Repeat at top and bottom. Press.

6. Border 2: Make 192 half-square triangle units using the various darks with the light. Stitch 56 units together for each side of quilt, reversing order at center as shown in whole-quilt diagram. Stitch units together with a **scant** ¼″ seam allowance. Press well. Lay border edge to edge with quilt and adjust to fit by making a few seams between units a bit deeper or shallower. Repeat for other side border. Repeat for top and bottom using 40 units for each, adding the 2″ light squares at each end. Press.

7. Border 3: Repeat Step 5. Press.

8. Piece backing vertically to same size as batting. Use your favorite layering, quilting, and binding methods to finish quilt.

1.

For One Block

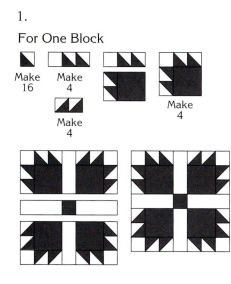

Make 16   Make 4   Make 4   Make 4

Make 4

2-4.

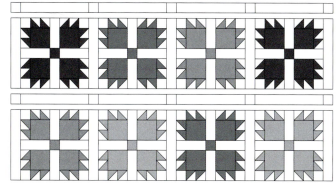

Potpourri

peel of ½ lemon
peel of ½ orange
2 bay leaves
½ c. whole cloves
4 small cinnamon sticks
1½ quarts water

Simmer gently, adding water as needed.

Photo on page 53
Finished sizes: 24″ swag, 8″ bow
Use 42-44″-wide fabric.

Yardage & Materials

Swag fabric – for 3	1⅝ yds.
Bow fabric – for 4	1⅜ yds.
Batting – thin cotton for 3 swags	3 rectangles 13x26″
Stuffing – for 4 bows	small amount

Cutting Patterns on pages 66-67

Swags	6
Bows	8 bows, 8 ties

Swag Directions

Use ¼″ seam allowance unless otherwise noted.

1. On right side of three swag sections, transfer the four curved stitching lines dividing the swag into segments.

2. Layer for each swag:
   a. batting
   b. marked swag piece, right side up
   c. unmarked swag piece, right side down

3. Stitch, leaving open as indicated on pattern. Trim batting even with swag pieces. Clip, turn, press, and slipstitch opening closed.

4. Topstitch ¼″ from edge around entire swag. Topstitch the four transferred lines.

Bow Directions

Use ¼″ seam allowance unless otherwise noted.

1. For each bow, stitch two bow pieces, right sides together, leaving open as indicated on pattern. Clip, turn, and press.

2. Stuff each end of rectangle with small amount of stuffing, using very little in center. Slipstitch opening closed.

3. For each tie, stitch two tie pieces right sides together, leaving an opening near center for turning. Clip, turn, and press.

4. Fold center section of tie in half lengthwise, then fold tie in half crosswise. See diagram on page 67. Stitch across tie 2¼″ from folded edge, forming a loop.

5. Insert bow into loop and pull seam slightly toward back.

6. Hang swags with a bow between them on wall with fine straight pins.

Photos on page 57 & front cover

Approximate finished size 58x64″

Use 42-44″-wide fabric. When strips appear in the cutting list, cut crossgrain strips (selvage to selvage).

Yardage

Assorted reds to total	1 yd.
Assorted greens to total	1 yd.
Assorted golds to total	¾ yd.
Background for Santas	⅝ yd.
Background for all star blocks	1 yd.
White for snow	¼ yd.
Black for light bulb bases	⅛ yd.
Other appliques – scraps	up to 4x8″
Narrow stripe for Borders 1 & 3	1⅝ yds.
Red & white for Border 4	½ yd. each
Border 5	1½ yds.
Backing	3⅞ yds.
Binding	⅝ yd.
Batting	64 x70″
Fusible bias tape – green	7 yds.

Cutting

Background for Santas	18½ x 24½″
Santa appliques	Patterns on pages 75-76
Snow	5½ x18½″

Border 1 (cut on lengthwise grain – extra length for mitering)
2 strips 3½ x 27″
2 strips 3½ x 33″

Border 2 (cutting is for one 6″ block)
Use two fabrics for each star & same background for all. Cut 8 red, 8 green, 6 gold blocks.

Star fabric #1	center	1 square – 3½″
Star fabric #2	points	4 squares – 2⅜″ – cut in half diagonally
Background		4 squares – 2⅜″ – cut in half diagonally
	corners	4 squares – 2″

Border 3 (cut on lengthwise grain – extra length for mitering)
2 strips 3½ x 44″
2 strips 3½ x 50″

Border 4	45 squares each Border 4 fabric – 2⅞″ cut in half diagonally
corners	4 squares – 2½″ white

Border 5	7 strips 6½″ wide
	52 light bulbs, 12 holly leaves, 12 berries – Pats. on p. 75
Binding	7 strips 2½″ wide

Directions

Use ¼″ seam allowance unless otherwise noted.

1. Trim top of snow piece with a gentle curve and applique to Santa background.

2. Stitch Border 1 strips to Santa background, centering from end to end and stopping stitching at seam intersections. Miter each corner using your favorite method. Press.

3. Applique Santas using your favorite method. Use photo and whole-quilt diagram as guides. We overlapped the star and the right Santa's hat onto Border 1.

4. Make 22 blocks for Border 2 following diagram and instructions in cutting chart. Press. Lay out blocks around Santa center, distributing color as desired. Stitch together the five

blocks for each side border and then stitch borders to quilt. Repeat with the six blocks for top and bottom.

5. Repeat Step 2 for Border 3.

6. Make Border 4:

a. Make 90 half-square triangle units.

b. Make two identical side borders of 24 units each following diagram.

c. Make two identical borders for top and bottom using 21 half-square triangle units with squares at each end. See diagram.

d. Stitch side borders to quilt using whole-quilt diagram as a guide for direction of red triangles.

e. Stitch top and bottom borders to quilt using whole-quilt diagram as a guide for direction of red triangles.

7. Press quilt well. Measure length of quilt. Piece border strips to the measured length and stitch to sides of quilt. Repeat at top and bottom. Press.

8. Cut a piece of fusible bias tape the width of the quilt. Pin bias tape to bottom border of quilt, matching centers. Working toward corner, curve one end of bias tape slightly down and then back up, having the top of the "up curve" even with the seam between Borders 3 and 4. Trim end of tape at center of corner where it will be covered by the holly leaves. Repeat at other end. Press bias tape to quilt. Repeat for other three sides of quilt. Curve will be gentler on sides of quilt.

9. Distribute bulbs along bias tape. Cover ends of bias tape with three holly leaves and three berries. Applique with your favorite method.

10. Piece backing horizontally to same size as batting. Use your favorite layering, quilting, and binding methods to finish quilt.

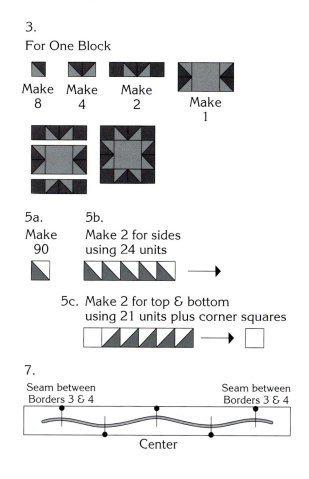

3.
For One Block

Make 8   Make 4   Make 2   Make 1

5a. Make 90   5b. Make 2 for sides using 24 units

5c. Make 2 for top & bottom using 21 units plus corner squares

7.
Seam between Borders 3 & 4   Seam between Borders 3 & 4

Center

Housewarming Soup

1 lb. boned chicken breast
8 c. chicken broth
1 onion, chopped
7 oz. mild green chiles, chopped
scraps of your favorite veggies

1 bay leaf
½ tsp. celery seed
¼ tsp. black pepper
salt to taste
8 oz. pasta, cooked

Combine chicken breast, broth, and onion in a large saucepan. Simmer 30 minutes. Remove chicken and cut into chunks. Return chicken to saucepan along with green chiles and spices. Add veggies such as celery, carrots, peas, corn, broccoli, tomatoes, black beans, hominy, mushrooms, black olives, and/or cauliflower. Simmer gently for 30-60 minutes, adding water if needed. Add cooked pasta to soup and serve. This recipe also works well with turkey breast, ground beef, ground turkey, or lean sausage.

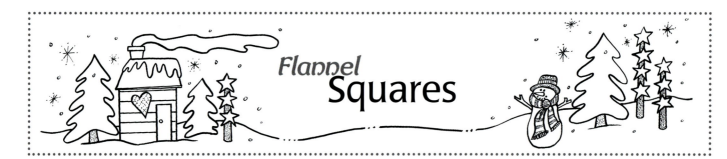

Flannel Squares

Photo on page 17

8½″ block – 48 blocks set 6 x 8

Approximate finished size 63 x 80″

Use 42-44″-wide fabric. When strips appear in the cutting list, cut crossgrain strips (selvage to selvage).

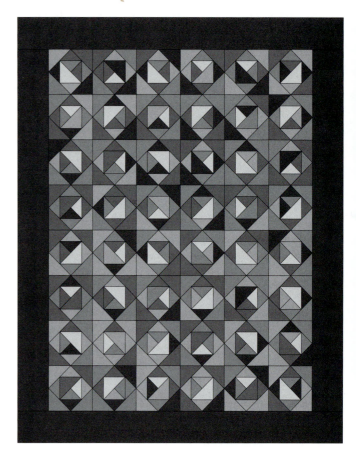

Yardage

Light flannels to total	¾ yds.
Medium & dark flannels to total	4½ yds.
Border	1½ yds.
Backing	5 yds.
Binding	⅔ yd.
Batting	69 x 86″

Cutting

A 12 light squares – 3⅞″ – cut in half diagonally

B 12 light squares – 5⅛″ – cut in half diagonally

A 132 medium & dark squares – 3⅞″ – cut in half diagonally

B 108 medium & dark squares – 5⅛″ – cut in half diagonally

Border 7 strips 6½″ wide

Binding 8 strips 2½″ wide

Directions

Use ¼″ seam allowance unless otherwise noted.

1. Make 48 blocks following diagram. Use one piece cut from the light scraps, either an A or a B, in each block. Press blocks.

2. Stitch blocks into eight rows of six, rotating as desired. Stitch rows together. Press.

3. Border: Measure length of quilt. Piece border strips to the measured length and stitch to sides of quilt. Repeat at top and bottom. Press.

4. Piece backing vertically to same size as batting. Use your favorite layering, quilting, and binding methods to finish quilt.

1.

2.
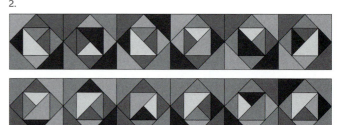

······Casserole Caddy·······

Photos on pages 21 & 29

For 8″ square casserole dish. Makes a great bread basket too!

Yardage

Prewash fabric and batting so caddy will fit after subsequent launderings.

Fabric	1⅛ yds.
Optional applique	scraps up to 5″ square
Batting – thin cotton	⅝ yd.
Heavy cardboard	

Cutting

Base	one 14″ square, one 15″ square
Center pocket	one rectangle 9x9½″
Side pockets	four rectangles 6x9″
Applique pieces	bird & star patterns on p. 46 & 54, holly patterns on page 76
Ties	eight 1½x12″ rectangles
Batting	15″ square
Cardboard	one 7¼″ square
	four 2x7¼″ rectangles

Directions

1. Layer in order and pin well:
   a. batting square
   b. large fabric square, right side up
   c. small fabric square, right side down, centered on others

2. Stitch around small square with a ⅜″ seam allowance, leaving 4″ open on one side for turning. Trim large squares even with small square. Clip corners. Turn through opening so batting is sandwiched between fabric layers. Press. Pin opening closed. Topstitch very close to entire outside edge of caddy.

3. Lightly mark a diagonal 2″ grid on outside of caddy and machine quilt on the lines.

4. Mark fold lines on inside of caddy, as shown, 2½″ from each side.

5. Optional: Applique holly on each side panel on outside of caddy, centered from side to side and about ½″ from outside edge.

6. Hem one 9″ side of center pocket piece: press ½″ to wrong side then press ½″ to wrong side again. Stitch close to fold. Pocket should measure 8½″ high by 9″ wide.

7. Optional: Applique chickadee and star on right side of pocket, centered, hem at top, using your favorite method.

8. Lay pocket wrong side down on inside of caddy, matching hemmed edge with one marked fold line. See diagram. Tuck under and pin the three raw edges to meet marked fold lines on caddy. Press pocket. Stitch pinned edges very close to folds.

9. Press the 1½x12″ pieces for ties in half lengthwise, wrong sides together. Unfold. Press long raw edges in to meet pressed line. See diagram. Fold in one end, then refold along center line. Stitch across end and along double-folded edge.

10. Press the four 6x9″ pieces for the side pockets in half lengthwise, wrong sides together. Pieces should measure 3x9″. Lay one side pocket on side of caddy with fold next to edge of center pocket. See diagram. Tuck under and pin the three raw edges to meet marked fold lines and outside edge of caddy. Press pocket. Repeat for other three side pockets.

11. Tuck raw end of a tie under corner of side pocket at each corner as shown. Pin in place. Stitch pinned edges of pockets, catching ties in stitching.

12. Trim cardboard pieces slightly, if necessary, to fit pockets. Slide cardboard pieces into pockets. Fold sides up and tie each corner in a bow.

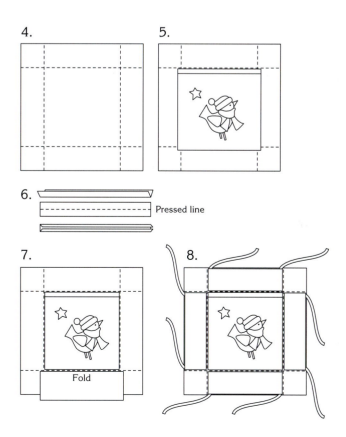

Stars

Photo on page 17

8″ block – 80 blocks set 8x10

Approximate finished size 76x92″

Use 42-44″-wide fabric. When strips appear in the cutting list, cut crossgrain strips (selvage to selvage).

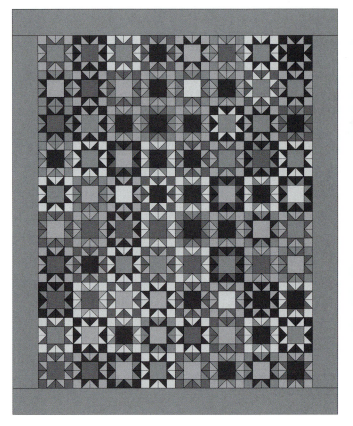

Yardage

Light flannels
creams & tans to total   4-5 yds.
Medium & dark flannels
reds & greens to total   4-5 yds.
Border   1¾ yds.
Backing   7 yds.
Binding   ¾ yd.
Batting   82x98″

Cutting

Cutting for one block (use three fabrics)
Background
  Corners   4 squares – 2½″
  Star point units   4 squares – 2⅞″ – cut in half diagonally
Star points   4 squares – 2⅞″ – cut in half diagonally
Star center   1 square – 4½″
Border   8 strips 6½″ wide
Binding   9 strips 2½″ wide

Directions

Use ¼″ seam allowance unless otherwise noted.

1. Make 80 blocks following diagram. Use three fabrics for each block, one for the background, one for the star points, and one for the star center. Vary the placement of light, medium, and dark from block to block. Some blocks will appear darker over all, and some will appear lighter. Some blocks will have high contrast among the three fabrics used, and others will have low contrast. See photo and whole-quilt diagram. Press blocks.

2. Stitch blocks into ten rows of eight. Stitch rows together. Press.

3. Border: Measure length of quilt. Piece border strips to the measured length and stitch to sides of quilt. Repeat at top and bottom. Press.

4. Piece backing horizontally to same size as batting. Use your favorite layering, quilting, and binding methods to finish quilt.

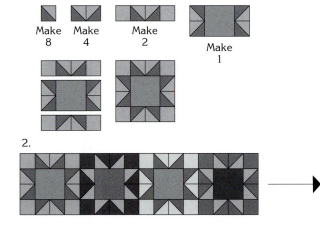

1. For One Block

Make 8   Make 4   Make 2   Make 1

2.

Photo on page 60

9½″ block – 48 blocks set 6x8

Approximate finished size 69x88″

Use 42-44″-wide fabric. When strips appear in the cutting list, cut crossgrain strips (selvage to selvage).

Yardage

Light flannel for center squares	⅓ yd.
Light flannels to total	4 yds.
Dark (& medium) flannels to total	4 yds.
Border	1¾ yds.
Backing	5½ yds.
Binding	¾ yd.
Batting	75x94″

Cutting

NOTE: Cut Pieces 1 & 2 from the same light fabric, Pieces 3 & 4 from the same dark fabric, and so on. See diagrams.

Centers		48 squares – 2½″
Lights	Piece 1	48 rectangles – 1¼ x 2½″
	Piece 2	48 rectangles – 1¼ x 3¼″
	Piece 5	48 rectangles – 1¼ x 4″
	Piece 6	48 rectangles – 1¼ x 4¾″
	Piece 9	48 rectangles – 1¼ x 5½″
	Piece 10	48 rectangles – 1¼ x 6¼″
	Piece 13	48 rectangles – 1¼ x 7″
	Piece 14	48 rectangles – 1¼ x 7¾″
	Piece 17	48 rectangles – 1¼ x 8½″
	Piece 18	48 rectangles – 1¼ x 9¼″
Darks	Piece 3	48 rectangles – 1¼ x 3¼″
	Piece 4	48 rectangles – 1¼ x 4″
	Piece 7	48 rectangles – 1¼ x 4¾″
	Piece 8	48 rectangles – 1¼ x 5½″
	Piece 11	48 rectangles – 1¼ x 6¼″
	Piece 12	48 rectangles – 1¼ x 7″
	Piece 15	48 rectangles – 1¼ x 7¾″
	Piece 16	48 rectangles – 1¼ x 8½″
	Piece 19	48 rectangles – 1¼ x 9¼″
	Piece 20	48 rectangles – 1¼ x 10″
Border		8 strips 6½″ wide
Binding		9 strips 2½″ wide

Directions

Use ¼″ seam allowance unless otherwise noted.

1. Make 48 blocks in five clockwise rounds following diagram. Pieces 1 and 2 are both the same light fabric; pieces 3 and 4 are both the same dark fabric; and so on. Press blocks.

2. Stitch blocks into eight rows of six, rotating them as shown. All rows are the same. Stitch rows together, rotating even rows 180° as shown. Press.

3. Border: Measure length of quilt. Piece border strips to the measured length and stitch to sides of quilt. Repeat for top and bottom. Press.

4. Piece backing vertically to same size as batting. Use your favorite layering, quilting, and binding methods to finish quilt.

1.

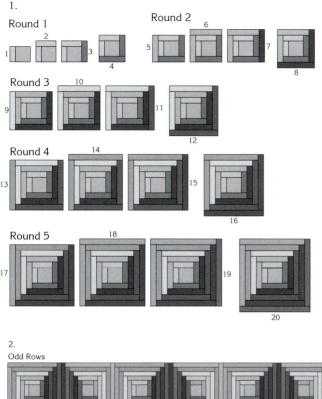

Round 1

Round 2

Round 3

Round 4

Round 5

2.

Odd Rows

Even Rows

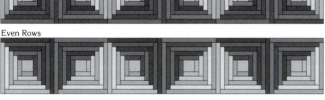

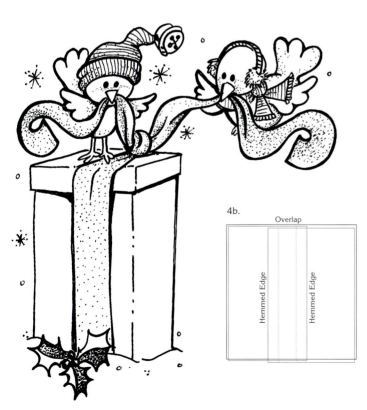

4b.

·······Log Cabin Pillow·······

Photo on page 60

Finished size 16″

Use 42-44″-wide fabric. When strips appear in the cutting list, cut crossgrain strips (selvage to selvage).

Yardage & Materials

Light flannel for center	scrap 3″ square
Light flannels	scraps up to 2x11″
Dark flannels	scraps up to 2x11″
Muslin (for optional quilting)	½ yd.
Border	¼ yd.
Envelope back	½ yd.
Binding	¼ yd.
Batting (for optional quilting)	18″ square
16″ pillow form	

Cutting

Light for center	1 square 2½″
Lights & darks	Use cutting chart on page 18, but cut only one each of pieces 1-20
Border	2 strips 3¾″ wide
Envelope backs	2 rectangles – 12x16½″
Binding	2 strips 2½ wide

Directions

Use ¼″ seam allowance unless otherwise noted.

1. Piece block using directions in Step 1 on page 18 and diagrams at left. Press.

2. Measure block. Cut side borders the measured length from one of the border strips. Stitch to sides of block. Repeat for top and bottom. Press.

3. Optional quilting: Cut muslin backing to same size as batting. Layer and quilt the pillow top. Trim backing and batting even with top.

4. Make envelope back:

   a. Hem one 16½″ side of each of the rectangles by pressing 1″ to the wrong side, then 1″ again, then topstitching close to fold.

   b. Lay two backing pieces, right sides up, on the wrong side of pillow front. Match raw edges, overlapping hemmed edges at center to create opening for envelope back. Baste outside edge with ¼″ seam allowance.

5. Stitch binding strips together end to end. Fold in half wrong sides together and stitch to right side of pillow with a ⅜″ seam allowance, mitering corners. Hand stitch to back at seamline.

19

Poinsettia & Holly Table Runner, Place Mats, Pot Holder, Casserole Caddy, & Apron   21

Photo on page 24

Approximate finished size 51x63"

Use 42-44"-wide fabric. When strips appear in the cutting list, cut crossgrain strips (selvage to selvage).

Yardage

Backgrounds – Backgrounds for snowman & lettering at right require 1⅝ yds. each if done without seaming. See cutting chart below for other background yardage requirements.

Snowman body & head	½ yd.
Snowman coat	¾ yd.
Snowman scarf	½ yd.
Snowman hat	⅜ yd.
Stocking cap	⅓ yd.
Lettering	¼ yd.
Scraps for other appliques	up to 15" square
Border 1	⅜ yd.
Border 2	¾ yd.
Backing	3½ yds.
Binding	½ yd.
Batting	57x69"

Buttons – two 1¼" for eyes, five ¾" for mouth, three 1" for coat, ten ½" for boots

Cutting

Backgrounds

1 – snowman	17½x54½"
2 – lettering at right	3½x54½"
3 – lettering at top	22½x3½"
4 – left snowflake	11½x9½"
5 – right snowflake	11½x9½"
6 – stocking cap	11½x8½"
7 – scarf	11½x8½"
8 – mittens	11½x9½"
9 – scarf	11½x9½"
10 – tree	8½x14½"
11 – tip of pipe	3½x4½"
12 – tip of carrot	3½x4½"
13 – heart	3½x6½"
14 – right-facing boot	11½x11½"
15 – pipe	11½x4½"
16 – carrot	11½x4½"
17 – left-facing boot	11½x12½"
18 – star	5½x5½"
19 – mug	6½x5½"

Appliques

Snowman's bottom section	17¼x10¼"
Snowman's coat	19½x29"
Snowman's top scarf	13½x7"
Snowman's bottom scarf	15x6½"
Snowman's sleeves	two 6" squares
Snowman's patches	two 6½" squares
Snowflakes*	Patterns on p. 55 & 63
Mug	Pattern on p. 77
Others	Patterns on p. 55, 58, 59, 71-74
Border 1	5 strips 2" wide
Border 2	6 strips 3½" wide
Binding	6 strips 2½" wide

*Refer to Step 3 on page 26 for paper folding.

......................Directions......................

Use ¼″ seam allowance unless otherwise noted.

NOTE: For ease in handling, some of the backgrounds could be appliqued before they are stitched together. See Step 1. These backgrounds are numbers 2, 3, 5, 8, 10, 13, 14, and 19.

1. Stitch backgrounds together following diagram, except for #2. It will be appliqued separately and stitched to quilt later, so snowman's bottom section and coat will be caught in seam. The dimensions of the backgrounds in the cutting chart are given **width** first to clarify how they fit into the quilt layout.

2. Diagrams at right are for the finished-size snowman bottom, coat and scarf pieces. Work from the right side of the fabric when cutting down the rectangles to these shapes. Add desired seam allowance if doing hand applique.

3. Line up right and bottom raw edges of snowman's bottom section with right and bottom raw edges of snowman background. Line up right raw edge of coat with right raw edge of snowman background. After positioning snowman's left sleeve, trim it even with right edge of snowman background. Applique quilt and lettering panel using your favorite method. Stitch lettering panel to quilt.

4. Border 1: Measure length of quilt. Piece border strips to the measured length and stitch to sides of quilt. Repeat at top and bottom. Press.

5. Border 2: Repeat Step 3. Press.

6. Piece backing horizontally to same size as batting. Use your favorite layering, quilting, and binding methods to finish quilt.

7. Sew buttons to quilt: eyes, mouth, coat, boots.

1.

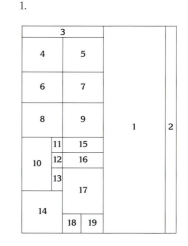

2.

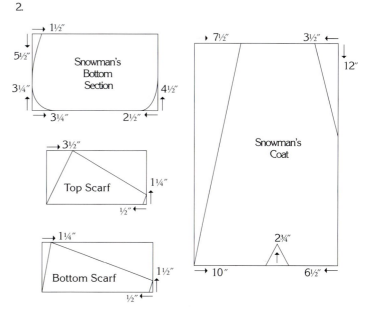

SEE THE MAGICAL WORLD OF SNOWFLAKES

The next time it snows, freeze sheets of black construction paper and catch snowflakes on them. When you come in from the cold, make hot cocoa and snuggle up under your Snowman quilt.

Hot Cocoa Mix

powdered milk – for making 8 quarts
16-oz. box chocolate drink mix
6-oz. jar of powdered coffee creamer
½ c. powdered sugar

Mix well and store in an airtight container. Stir ⅓ cup of mix into 6-8 oz. of hot water.

Marshmallow Floaters

Roll large marshmallows as flat as possible. Cut with small cookie cutters. Float them in your cocoa!

24   In the Meadow We Can Build a Snowman

Let It
Snow

Photo on page 25

6″ squares set around 42x60″ center panel

Approximate finished size 54x72″

Use 42-44″-wide fabric. When strips appear in the cutting list, cut crossgrain strips (selvage to selvage).

Yardage

Light flannels – 5 different ones	⅞ yd. each
Snowflakes – up to 22	
white-on-white scraps	12″ squares
Backing	3⅝ yds.
Binding	⅝ yd.
Batting	60x78″

Cutting

From each flannel	1 rectangle – 12½x42½″
	8 squares – 6½″ (38 needed)
Snowflakes	See Step 3. Patterns on p. 63
Binding	7 strips 2½″ wide

Directions

Use ¼″ seam allowance unless otherwise noted.

1. Stitch the five large rectangles together for center panel of quilt. Press.

2. Border: Stitch 6″ squares into two rows of ten. Adjust to fit quilt center, if necessary, by making seams between squares deeper or shallower. Stitch to sides of quilt. Make two rows of nine squares and stitch to top and bottom. Press.

3. To make each snowflake pattern, fold an 11″ square of paper in half, in half again, then in thirds. Reduce bulk by making the last two folds accordion-style, one-third in one direction, and one-third in the other. See diagram. Make a mark on the outside segment and open out the paper. Lay marked segment over one of the patterns on page 63, lining up the dotted lines on the folds. Trace solid lines only. Refold with tracing on outside and cut out on line. Applique snowflakes to quilt top with your favorite method, using whole-quilt diagram as a guide. We used nine small and thirteen medium and large snowflakes, repeating a few.

4. Piece backing horizontally to same size as batting. Use your favorite layering, quilting, and binding methods to finish quilt.

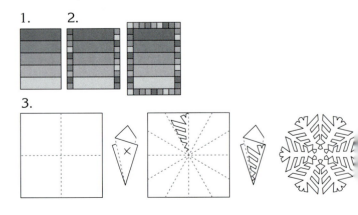

·········Noel Pillows·········

Photo on page 29

Finished size 16″

Use 42-44″-wide fabric. When strips appear in the cutting list, cut crossgrain strips (selvage to selvage).

Yardage & Materials

Letters	sky	⅜ yd.
	ground	⅜ yd.
Other appliques		scraps up to 5x9″
Fronts & envelope backs		2½ yds.
Binding		⅝ yd.
16″ pillow forms		4

Cutting

Applique pieces	Patterns on pages 71-74
Fronts	4 squares – 16½″
Envelope backs	8 rectangles – 12x16½″
Binding	7 strips 2½″ wide

Directions

Use ¼″ seam allowance unless otherwise noted.

1. Using your favorite applique method, make the four blocks using the diagrams and photos as guides. Press.

2. Make envelope backs:

   a. Hem one 16½″ side of each of the eight rectangles by pressing 1″ to the wrong side, then 1″ again, then topstitching close to fold.

   b. Lay two backing pieces, right sides up, on the wrong side of one of the pillow fronts. Match raw edges, overlapping hemmed edges at center, to create opening for envelope back. Baste outside edge with ¼″ seam allowance.

   c. Repeat with other three pillow fronts and their backings.

3. Stitch binding strips together end to end. Cut into four equal pieces. Fold one piece of binding in half wrong sides together and stitch to pillow with a ⅜″ seam allowance, mitering corners. Hand stitch to back at seamline.

2.

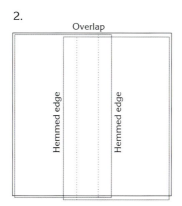

Overlap

Hemmed edge

Hemmed edge

Noel Pillows, Santa Place Mats, Chickadee Napkins, Casserole Caddy, Paper Gift Bag, & Place Cards   29

Christmas Card
Holder

Photos on page 61 & back cover

6″ block set with 1½″ sashing

Approximate finished size 16 x 31″

Use 42-44″-wide fabric. When strips appear in the cutting list, cut crossgrain strips (selvage to selvage).

·············· Yardage ··············

Appliques	scraps up to 5″ sq.
Blocks, pocket lining, border	1 yd.
Lettering	⅛ yd.
Sashing	⅙ yd.
Backing	¾ yd.
Binding	⅓ yd.
Batting	20 x 35″

·············· Cutting ··············

Applique pieces	Patterns on p. 68-69, 71-74
Blocks & pocket linings	9 squares – 6½″
Sashing	2 strips 2″ wide
Border	3 strips 4″ wide
Binding	3 strips 2½″ wide

·············· Directions ··············

Use ¼″ seam allowance unless otherwise noted.

1. Using your favorite applique method, make the three blocks. There will be six 6½″ squares left for pocket linings and the plain blocks beneath the pockets. Press.

2. Make a pocket with each appliqued block by stitching a pocket lining, right sides together, to it. Flip lining to back and press seam. Stitch lining to seam allowance (understitch).

3. Make pocket strip, referring to diagrams:

   a. Cut two 6½″ segments off each sashing strip and set remainder of strips aside.

   b. Stitch one 6½″ sashing strip to top of a plain block, right sides together. Flip strip over and press.

   c. Pin Santa block, right side up, over plain block, raw edges even, then lay a 6½″ sashing strip right side down on Santa block. Stitch. Flip strip over and press.

   d. Stitch a plain block to the bottom sashing strip, right sides together. Flip and press. Lay the tree block over the plain block and a sashing strip over that, as in Step 3c. Stitch.

   e. Repeat Step 3d with snowman block. Press well.

4. Measure length of pocket strip and cut remaining sashing strips to that length. Stitch to sides of pocket strip. Press.

5. Cut two 9½″ segments from one border strip. Stitch to top and bottom of quilt. Press. Measure length of quilt and cut remaining border strips to this length. Stitch to sides of quilt. Press.

30

6. Applique stars and letters to border using your favorite method.

7. Cut backing to same size as batting. Use your favorite layering, quilting, and binding methods to finish quilt.

2.

3b.

Pocket lining on top of appliqued block

Plain block

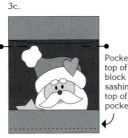

3c.

Pocket on top of plain block with sashing on top of pocket

3c.

Pocket is stitched only at bottom

3d.

Plain block

4.

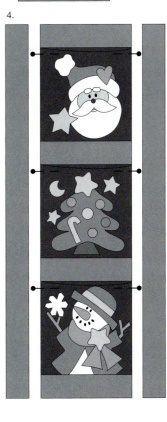

Photos on pages 21 & 61

Child's Snowman Apron – patterns on page 68
Child's Santa Apron – patterns on page 70
Adult Tall Santa Apron – patterns on pages 75 & 70
Adult Poinsettia Apron – patterns on page 76

Yardage & Materials

Purchased or premade aprons
Fabric scraps for applique

Cutting

Cut applique pieces as desired using photos as guides for color.

Directions

Applique with your favorite method using photos and diagrams as guides for placement. Stem on poinsettia apron is fusible bias tape.

32   Trees & Stars Quilt & Pillows, Poinsettia Stocking, Holly Berry Tree Skirt, & Basket Liner
Photo index page 3

Basket Liner

Photo on page 32
Use 42-44″-wide fabric.

Yardage & Materials

Round/oval basket – straight sides, small handle

Main fabric – can be prequilted muslin	1-2 yds. (will vary)
Lining	1-2 yds. (will vary)
Appliques – red & green	scraps 2x3½″
Prairie points – red & green	scraps 4″ square
Bows – two	¼ yd.
Batting – not needed if using prequilted muslin for main fabric	piece larger than bottom of basket

Cutting

Main fabric & lining	See Steps 2-3
Applique pieces	Patterns on page 76
Prairie points	3½″ squares
Bows	two rectangles 3½x40″

Directions

Use ¼″ seam allowance unless otherwise noted.

1. Set basket on piece of paper larger than bottom of basket. Trace around bottom of basket. Cut out pattern. Test size by pushing pattern down into basket. Pattern should be about ½″ bigger than inside bottom of basket to allow for seam allowance. Alter pattern if necessary.

2. If using prequilted muslin, cut one of main fabric and one of lining from pattern. Place pieces wrong sides together and baste outside edge.

   If using a main fabric that is not prequilted, cut out one piece of main fabric and one of lining larger than bottom of basket. Layer with batting and quilt in a crosshatch pattern. Cut out quilted basket bottom using paper pattern.

3. Measure from inside bottom of basket, up side, over edge, and down the outside three or four inches (Side A). Measure top edge of basket on outside edge from handle to handle (Side B). Cut two rectangles of fabric and two of lining using these measurements (Side A x Side B).

4. Make prairie points as shown. Arrange prairie points along one Side B on each main fabric rectangle, facing in. Start and end just inside Side A seam allowances. Use enough prairie points so they overlap at least ½″. Slip point of one inside the next. Pin and then baste to seam allowance.

5. Place each main fabric rectangle right sides together with a lining rectangle and stitch around three sides, leaving Side B opposite the prairie points open. Clip corners, turn, press. Baste open side closed.

6. Applique holly leaves and berries just above prairie points on main fabric side of each piece.

7. Pin side rectangles to basket bottom, right sides together, overlapping them as needed at position directly below handle. Place liner in basket and alter pinning, if necessary, to make liner fit around handle. Stitch.

8. Fold tie pieces lengthwise, right sides together. Cut 60° angles at each end. Stitch as shown, leaving a 2″ opening for turning at center on long side. Clip corners. Turn right side out. Press. Slipstitch opening closed.

9. Place liner in basket with prairie points and appliques folded over to outside. Tie bows to handles.

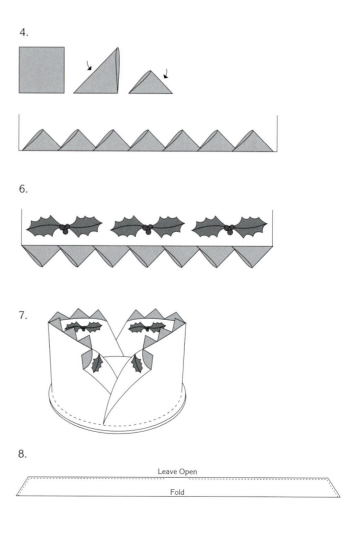

4.

6.

7.

8.

Leave Open

Fold

Photo on page 53. Makes a great tablecloth too!

Approximate finished size 49″

Use 42-44″-wide fabric. When strips appear in the cutting list, cut crossgrain strips (selvage to selvage).

Yardage

Background	¾ yd.
Dark #1 (red)	¾ yd.
Dark #2 (green)	¾ yd.
Medium #1 (red)	¼ yd.
Medium #2 (green)	¾ yd.
Backing (nondirectional)	2 yds.
Tree skirt binding	⅞ yd.
Tablecloth binding	⅝ yd.
Batting	54″ square (optional: flannel or very thin batting for tablecloth)

Cutting

NOTE: Rotary cutting rulers needed are a 6x24″ with eighth-inch and 45° markings and a 12″ square.

Background	(for triangles)	6 squares – 11½″ – cut in **quarters** diagonally
Dark #1	(for diamonds)	1 strip – 5⅝″
	(for triangles)	2 squares – 11½″ – cut in **quarters** diagonally
Dark #2	(for diamonds)	3 strips – 5⅝″
Medium #1	(for diamonds)	1 strip – 5⅝″
Medium #2	(for diamonds)	3 strips – 5⅝″
Binding		
Inside circle of tree skirt		2½ x 26″ **bias** strip
Binding		
Outside of tree skirt or tablecloth		6 strips 2½″ wide

Directions for Tree Skirt

Use ¼″ seam allowance unless otherwise noted.

1. Cut all 5⅝″ strips into diamonds (4 per strip). Make first cut with 45° marking on ruler. Make second and third cuts 5⅝″ parallel to previous cuts. See diagram.

2. Piece center star with alternating Dark #1 and Medium #1 diamonds. Stitch to edge of fabric at center but only to seam intersections at outer edge where triangles will be set in. Backstitch at these seam intersections.

3. Make four half-square triangle units with background and Dark #1 triangles. Set in the four squares at every other "gap", background triangle toward center of star. Set in background triangles at remaining "gaps", forming a large square. See diagram.

4. Make four side units. Stitch only to seam intersections and backstitch where indicated on diagram.
   a. Make four: Dark #2—Medium #2—Dark #2.
   b. Make four: Medium #2—Dark #2—Medium #2.
   c. Set in background triangles as shown.
   d. Stitch together one from Step 4a and one from Step 4b as shown, then set in a Dark #1 triangle.

5. Stitch side units to center square, stitching only to seam intersections where indicated. Stitch remaining four seams from outside edge of tree skirt to corners of center square, stitching only to seam intersections where indicated. Press well.

6. Draw a 6″ circle on right side of tree skirt at center. Draw a line from edge of center circle to outside edge of tree skirt as shown.

7. Piece backing as shown. Layer and baste tree skirt with backing and batting. Using an even-feed foot, stitch ⅛″ to each side of center back line and around circle at center.

8. Quilt tree skirt as desired. Cut between two stitching lines at center back then cut out center circle just inside stitching line.

9. Fold bias strip wrong sides together; stitch to right side of center circle with ⅜″ seam allowance. Trim ends even with raw edges at center back. Make one long piece of binding with other six strips; fold in half wrong sides together. Starting at center circle, and leaving ½″ extending, stitch to center back, outer edge, and other side of center back, mitering corners and leaving ½″ extending at end. Fold in extensions at center before folding binding to back for hand stitching.

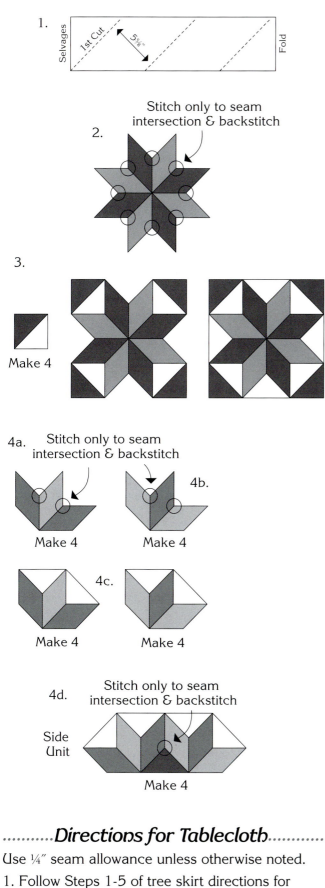

1.

Selvages | 1st Cut | 5⅝" | Fold

2.

Stitch only to seam intersection & backstitch

3.

Make 4

4a.

Stitch only to seam intersection & backstitch

4b.

Make 4   Make 4

4c.

Make 4   Make 4

4d.

Stitch only to seam intersection & backstitch

Side Unit

Make 4

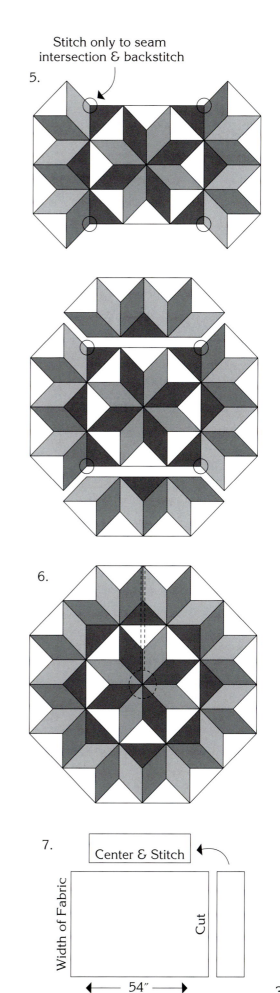

Stitch only to seam intersection & backstitch

5.

6.

7.

Center & Stitch

Width of Fabric

Cut

← 54" →

..........*Directions for Tablecloth*..........

Use ¼" seam allowance unless otherwise noted.

1. Follow Steps 1-5 of tree skirt directions for piecing the tablecloth.

2. Use your favorite layering, quilting, and binding methods to finish tablecloth.

35

Holly Berry
Tree Skirt

Photo on page 32. Makes a great tablecloth too!

Approximate finished size 54″

Use 42-44″-wide fabric.

Yardage

Prequilted double-faced muslin	3¼ yds.
Leaves – greens to total	1½ yds.
Berries	⅛ yd.
Binding	⅞ yd.
Fusible bias tape for stem	4½ yds.

Cutting

Applique pieces – Patterns on page 65. Cut 32 holly leaves, 27 berries, 11 oak leaves, and 4 maple leaves. Reverse some for variety.

Binding – **bias** strips 2½″ wide to make 280″ length for tree skirt, 180″ length for tablecloth

Directions for Tree Skirt

Use ¼″ seam allowance unless otherwise noted.

1. Cut length of quilted muslin in half and stitch the two pieces together along the selvage edges. Press seam open. Lay on carpeted floor right side up.

2. Stick a large pin straight through the center of the muslin into the carpet. Tie a 36″ length of string to the pin, then tie the string around a pencil 27″ from the pin. See diagram. Mark a 54″ circle on the muslin with the string compass. Move pencil and mark another circle for the center hole that is 6″ in diameter. Mark back center line from small circle to large circle 90° from seams in muslin, as shown.

3. Staystitch both circles and ⅛″ from each side of center back line. Cut out just outside staystitching of the 54″ circle.

4. Mark tree skirt for placement of bias stem:

   a. Pinmark edge of tree skirt in fourths, then eighths, then sixteenths, as shown.

   b. From every other pin, measure 6″ in from outer edge toward center and pinmark. From the other eight marks, measure in 10″ toward center and pinmark.

   c. Starting at center back, curve bias from one pin to the next and use transparent tape to hold it in place. Press stem to tree skirt, removing tape as you go.

5. Place leaves and berries as desired along stem. We grouped three holly leaves with three berries at nine evenly spaced spots, then filled in with other leaves. Applique leaves, berries, and stem using your favorite method.

6. Cut tree skirt between stitching lines at center back. Cut out center circle just inside stitching line.

7. Stitch binding strips together end to end. Fold in half wrong sides together and stitch to right side of tree skirt with a ⅜″ seam allowance, mitering corners. Hand stitch to back at seamline.

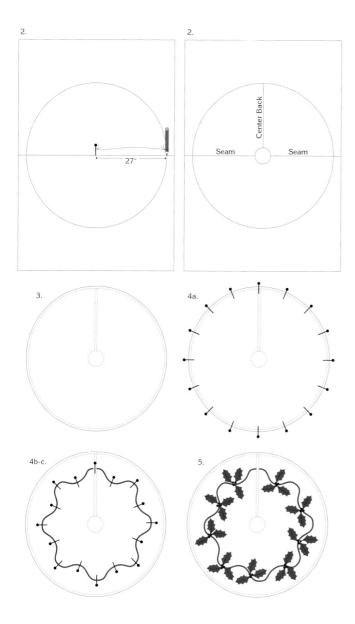

·····Poinsettia Stocking·····

Photo on page 32   Finished length 20″

Yardage

Prequilted double-faced muslin   ½ yd.
Appliques – red & green scraps   up to 5x6″
Binding   ⅓ yd.
Fusible bias tape – green   12″

Cutting Patterns on pages 62 & 76

Muslin   1 socking, 1 stocking reversed
Applique pieces   1 toe, 1 heel, 7 poinsettia petals, 7 circles, 6 holly leaves & 6 berries
Binding – bias   2½″ wide, pieced to 70″ long

Directions

1. Applique stocking front with your favorite method using photo and diagram as guides for placement. Stem is fusible bias tape. Reverse some holly leaves for variety.

2. Press binding strips in half lengthwise, wrong sides together. Bind top edges of stocking front and back using a ⅜″ seam allowance.

3. Pin stocking front and back wrong sides together. Baste ¼″ from edge.

4. Bind raw edges with a ⅜″ seam allowance, leaving a 6″ tail at top left to make hanger and folding end to inside at top right.

5. For hanger, stitch folded edges of binding tail together. Fold raw end under on back of stocking and stitch in place.

··········Directions for Tablecloth··········

Use ¼″ seam allowance unless otherwise noted.

1. Follow Step 1 of tree skirt directions.

2. Stick a large pin straight through the center of the muslin into the carpet. Tie a 36″ length of string to the pin, then tie the string around a pencil 27″ from the pin. See diagram. Mark a 54″ circle on the muslin with the string compass.

3. Staystitch circle and cut out just outside stitching.

4. Follow Steps 4-5 of tree skirt directions. Cover raw ends of bias tape with an applique piece.

5. Stitch binding strips together end to end. Fold in half wrong sides together and stitch to right side of tablecloth with a ⅜″ seam allowance. Hand stitch to back at seamline.

Photo on page 49
Approximate finished size 11x32″

Use 42-44″-wide fabric.

Yardage

Background	½ yd.
Snow – snowman versions	⅛ yd.
Appliques – scraps	up to 5x14″
Muslin for quilting & backing	⅞ yd.
Binding	⅓ yd.
Batting	14x34″
Poster board	1 piece

Cutting

Background – one rectangle 14x34″
Snow applique piece – one rectangle 3½x34″
Other applique pieces – Patterns on pages 46-48,
   50-51, 54
Muslin – two rectangles 14x34″
Binding – **bias** strips 2½″ wide to make 80″ length
Poster board – use line indicated on pattern piece,
   page 54

Directions

Use ¼″ seam allowance unless otherwise noted.

1. Make full-sized background arch pattern (page 54). Cut out pattern on outside line. Lay on right side of background rectangle and draw a line around it.

2. Cut a gentle curve on top edge of snow rectangle if making one of the snowman versions. Applique chosen design using your favorite method.

3. Layer appliqued piece with batting and one of the muslin rectangles. Quilt as desired. Cut out on line drawn in Step 1.

4. Cut out a muslin backing using quilted piece as a pattern. Hem bottom of muslin arch with a ¾″ single hem.

5. Baste hemmed muslin and quilted piece, wrong sides together, along curved edge, leaving hemmed edge free.

6. Stitch binding strips together end to end. Cut off a piece 35″ long. Fold in half wrong sides together and stitch to right side of bottom edge of Door Topper with a ⅜″ seam allowance. Trim raw ends even with Topper. Hand stitch to back at seamline. Bind curved edge, folding in raw ends at corners.

7. Slide poster board into pocket. Blind hem bottom edge of muslin to backing of quilted piece or tack at intervals.

8. Hang on wall above door with fine straight pins.

·····Santa Place Mats·····

Photo on page 29   Finished size 14x18″

Use 42-44″-wide fabric. When strips appear in the cutting list, cut crossgrain strips (selvage to selvage).

Yardage For two

Main fabric	½ yd.
Appliques	scraps up to 7x9½″
Backing	½ yd.
Binding	⅜ yd.
Batting – thin cotton	2 rectangles 16x20″

Cutting For two

Main fabric	2 rectangles 14x18″
Applique pieces	Patterns on page 46
Backing	2 rectangles 16x20″
Binding	4 strips 2½″ wide

Directions

Use ¼″ seam allowance unless otherwise noted.

1. Applique Santa on main fabric rectangle using your favorite method. Line up raw bottom edge of suit with bottom edge of rectangle so it will be caught in binding.

2. Layer:
   a. backing, wrong side up
   b. batting
   c. appliqued piece, right side up

   Quilt as desired. Trim even with appliqued piece.

3. Stitch binding strips together end to end. Fold in half wrong sides together and stitch to right side of place mat with a ⅜″ seam allowance, mitering corners. Hand stitch to back at seamline.

·····Chickadee Napkins·····

Photo on page 29   Finished size 16″

Use 42-44″-wide fabric.

Yardage For two

Napkin	½ yd.
Appliques	scraps up to 5″ square

Directions

1. Cut two 16½″ squares for napkins.

2. Stitch ¼″ double hems on each side.

3. Cut out appliques using patterns on pages 46 and 54.

4. Applique a chickadee and a star in corner of each napkin, using your favorite method.

····Trees & Stars Pillows····

Photo on page 32   Approximate finished size 11″

Use 42-44″-wide fabric. When strips appear in the cutting list, cut crossgrain strips (selvage to selvage).

Yardage & Materials For one pillow

Background & back	¾ yd.
Tree or star	scraps up to 4x7″
Muslin (for optional quilting)	½ yd.
Binding	¼ yd.
Batting (for optional quilting)	13″ square
Needlepunch (for pillow form)	two 12″ squares
Stuffing (for pillow form)	1 lb.

Cutting

Tree
  Background

center units	4 squares – 3⁵⁄₁₆″
sides	1 square – 4⅞″ – cut in half diagonally
trunk units	2 rectangles 3¼x8″
corner triangles	2 squares – 6½″ cut in half diagonally

  Tree fabric

center unit	2 rectangles 3⁵⁄₁₆x6³⁄₁₆″
tree top	1 square – 4⅞″ – cut in half diagonally (1 extra)
Trunk	1 rectangle 1⅜x8″

Star
  Background

corners	4 squares – 3½″
side units	4 rectangles – 2½x3½″
corner triangles	2 squares – 6½″ cut in half diagonally

  Star fabric

center	1 square – 2½″
points	Pattern on page 76 4 & 4 reversed
Envelope back	2 rectangles – 10x11¾″
Binding	2 strips 2½″ wide

Directions

Use ¼″ seam allowance unless otherwise noted.

1. Piece block using directions in Step 1 or 2 on page 6 and diagrams on page 7. Stitch corner triangles to block. Press.

2. Refer to Steps 3-5 on page 19, hemming 11¾″ sides of envelope back rectangles in Step 4a.

3. Make pillow form: Stitch needlepunch squares together, leaving a 4″ opening on one side for stuffing. Turn, stuff. Stitch opening closed.

....Gathered Tree Skirt....

Photo on page 60

Approximate finished size 48″

Use 42-44″-wide fabric.

Yardage & Materials

Main fabric	2½ yds.
Border print with 3″ motif (must be able to cut 6½″ wide strips)	171″ of stripe
Narrow ribbon or cording	2 yds.

Cutting

Main fabric – cut yardage in half lengthwise & cut off selvages

Border print – cut enough strips 6½″ wide to make finished piece 171″ long – plan a 3″ motif with a ¼″ seam allowance to one side and a 3¼″ facing to the other side

Directions for Tree Skirt

Use ¼″ seam allowance unless otherwise noted.

1. Stitch the two large rectangles of the main fabric end to end to make a piece approximately 22 x 171″. Zigzag edges of seam allowances if desired.

2. Stitch border strips together end to end to make a piece 171″ long. Press seams open; press strip in half lengthwise, wrong sides together.

3. Stitch border strip to main fabric rectangle, right sides together, three raw edges even. Zigzag raw edges of seam allowance. Press so seam allowance falls away from border.

4. Make narrow double hems on the two short ends of the tree skirt (the center back).

5. Make a casing on the long raw edge by pressing ¾″ then ¾″ again to wrong side and stitching close to fold.

6. Thread ribbon on a needle with a large eye (or attach to a bodkin) and run it through the casing, gathering as you go.

7. Draw up tree skirt around tree trunk and tie ribbon in a bow. Trim ribbon ends to desired length.

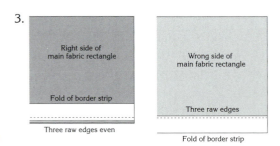

3.
Right side of main fabric rectangle
Fold of border strip
Three raw edges even

Wrong side of main fabric rectangle
Three raw edges
Fold of border strip

....Matching Ornaments....

Photo on page 60   Seam allowance ¼″

Stocking Materials For five 5½″ ornaments

Main fabric	⅜ yd.
Border print with 1½″ motif (must be able to cut 3½″ wide strip)	40″ of stripe
Narrow ribbon for hangers	1¼ yds.
Stuffing	small amount
Berries, cinnamon sticks, &/or greenery	

Stocking Directions

1. Cut five stockings and five reversed from main fabric. Pattern on page 62. From border print, cut one strip 3½″ wide, planning a 1½″ motif with a ¼″ seam allowance to one side and a 1¾″ facing to the other side.

2. Stitch stockings, right sides together, leaving tops open. Turn right side out.

3. Cut border strip into five 8″ segments. For each stocking cuff, fold one segment in half, right sides together, and stitch across short end, forming a ring. Press seam open. Fold ring in half, wrong sides together.

4. Slip cuff into stocking, right side of cuff facing wrong side of stocking, seam in cuff matched to back seam of stocking. Pin. Stitch. Fold cuff to outside; seam at top edge. Stuff lightly.

5. Cut five 8″ pieces of ribbon. Tie ends in knot and tack to inside of stocking at back seam. Fill with berries, cinnamon sticks and/or greenery.

Cinnamon Bag Materials

For five 3½ x 5½″ ornaments

Fabric	⅓ yd.
Stuffing	small amount
Fabric for ties	⅛ yd.
Narrow ribbon for hangers	1¼ yds.
Jingle bells, berries, cinnamon sticks, &/or greenery	

Cinnamon Bag Directions

1. Cut five 7½ x 8″ rectangles. Press 1″ hem on 8″ edge (top) of each rectangle. Stitch ⅝″ from fold.

2. Fold in half, right sides together. Stitch side and bottom edges with ¼″ seam allowance. Clip corners, turn, press.

3. Stuff loosely. Fill with berries, cinnamon sticks, and/or greenery. Fringe edges of 1½ x 12″ fabric rectangles and tie around bag. Tack jingle bells close to knot.

4. Make hangers as in Step 5 above.

Poinsettia & Holly Place Mats

Photo on page 21   Finished size 14x18″

Use 42-44″-wide fabric. When strips appear in the cutting list, cut crossgrain strips (selvage to selvage).

Yardage For two

Prequilted muslin	½ yd.
Appliques – red & green	scraps up to 3x5″
Backing	½ yd.
Binding	⅜ yd.

Cutting For two. Patterns on page 76.

Muslin	2 rectangles 14x18″
Applique pieces	7 petals, 7 circles, & 2 holly leaves for each poinsettia OR 3 holly leaves & 3 berries for each holly cluster
Backing	2 rectangles 14x18″
Binding	4 strips 2½″ wide

Directions

Use ¼″ seam allowance unless otherwise noted.

1. Applique poinsettia or holly cluster to top left corner of each prequilted muslin rectangle using your favorite method.

2. Layer a place mat front wrong sides together with a backing rectangle and pin the edges.

3. Stitch binding strips together end to end. Fold in half wrong sides together and stitch to right side of place mat with a ⅜″ seam allowance, mitering corners. Hand stitch to back at seamline.

Poinsettia & Holly Pot Holders

Photo on page 21   Finished size 8″

Yardage For two pot holders

Prequilted muslin	⅓ yd.
Appliques – red & green	scraps up to 3x5″
Backing	⅓ yd.
Binding	¼ yd.
Batting – dense cotton	2 squares 8″

Cutting For two. Patterns on page 76.

Muslin & backing	2 squares each – 8″
Applique pieces	see place mat cutting above
Binding	2 strips 2½″ wide

Directions

Use place mat directions above, placing batting between pot holder front and backing when layering.

Poinsettia & Holly Table Runner

Photo on page 21   Finished size 14x54″

Use 42-44″-wide fabric. When strips appear in the cutting list, cut crossgrain strips (selvage to selvage).

Yardage

Prequilted muslin	1⅝ yds.
Appliques – red & green	scraps up to 3x5″
Backing	⅞ yd.
Binding	⅜ yd.
Fusible bias tape	1½ yds.

Cutting Patterns on page 76

Muslin	1 rectangle 14x54″
Applique pieces	21 poinsettia petals, 21 circles 14 holly leaves, 18 berries
Backing	2 strips 14″ wide
Binding	4 strips 2½″ wide

Directions

Use ¼″ seam allowance unless otherwise noted.

1. Pin fusible bias tape in a gentle curve along center of muslin rectangle. Trim so it ends 6″ from each end of table runner.

2. Place three poinsettias, holly leaves, and berries along stem as desired. Applique using your favorite method.

3. Piece backing to 14x54″. Layer runner wrong sides together with backing and pin the edges.

4. Stitch binding strips together end to end. Fold in half wrong sides together and stitch to right side of table runner with a ⅜″ seam allowance, mitering corners. Hand stitch to back at seamline.

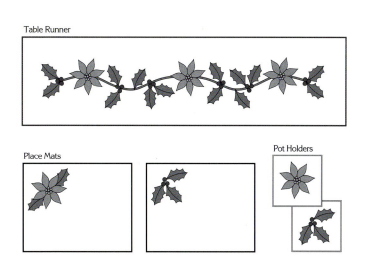

Gift Bags

Photo on page 61   Finished size 10x13x4¼″
Use 42-44″-wide fabric.

Yardage

Block background – scrap	8″ square
Appliques – scraps	up to 4″ sq.
Block borders – 11 scrap strips	1½x12″
Handles	⅙ yd.
Main fabric for bag	½ yd.
Lining	½ yd.
Paper-backed fusible web	1 yd.

Cutting

Block background	1 square 6½″
Applique pieces	Pattern on page 69 (or Snowman p. 68 or Santa p. 69)
Block borders	11 rectangles 1½x12″
Handles	2 rectangles 4x18½″
Main fabric	1 rectangle 2¾x30½″
	2 rectangles 10½x13½″

Directions

Use ¼″ seam allowance unless otherwise noted.

1. Applique the block using your favorite method.

2. Stitch 1½x12″ strips to the top and bottom, trimming off excess length. Stitch 1½x12″ strips to the sides, trimming off excess length. Repeat at top and bottom, then sides. Stitch one 1½x12″ strip to the bottom and two 1½x12″ strips to the top, trimming as before. Press front panel well.

3. Stitch 10½x13½″ rectangles to each side of front panel. Stitch 2¾x30½″ rectangle to bottom. Press.

4. Lay wrong side of bag on adhesive side of fusible web and cut out web to same size. Fuse to wrong side of bag following manufacturer's directions. Peel off backing. Lay wrong side of bag on wrong side of lining fabric and fuse. Cut lining even with bag.

5. Fold bag in half, right sides together, and stitch center back seam.

6. Fold bag so center back seam is aligned with center front. Stitch across bottom of bag.

7. For boxed bottom, refold one corner at bottom of bag to match diagram. Measure 2¼″ from corner and draw a line perpendicular to seam. Stitch on line. Repeat at other corner. Turn bag right side out.

8. Press a ¼″ hem to inside of bag at top edge. Topstitch ⅛″ from fold. Press sides of bag following diagram.

9. Press the handles in half lengthwise, wrong sides together. Unfold. Press long raw edges in to meet pressed line. Refold along center line. Stitch along both long edges. Topstitch ends of one handle to inside of bag 1″ in from sides of bag front. Repeat with other handle on bag back.

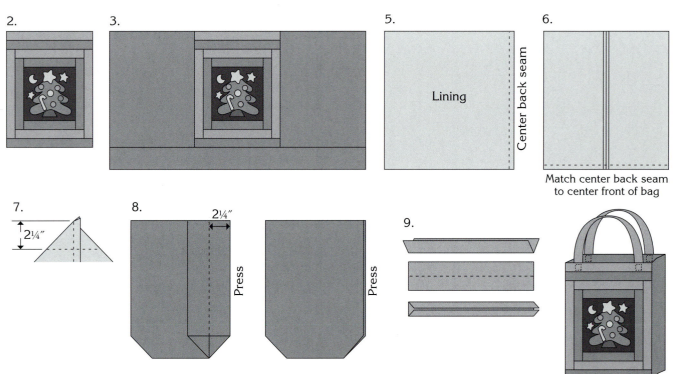

·········· Wine Bags ··········

Photo on page 61   Finished size 4x17x3½″
Use 42-44″-wide fabric.

Yardage & Materials

Appliques – scraps	up to 3½x10″
Main fabric for bag	½ yd.
Lining	½ yd.
Paper-backed fusible web	⅝ yd.

Cutting

Applique pieces	Use any Tall Santa pattern, pages 75, 76
Main fabric	1 rectangle 20x15½″
Lining	1 rectangle 20x15½″
Fusible web	1 rectangle 20x15½″

Directions

Use ¼″ seam allowance unless otherwise noted.

1. Using your favorite method, applique one of the Santas to the main fabric rectangle, centered from right to left and 2½″ up from one of the 15½″ sides (bottom of bag).

2. Lay fusible web on wrong side of main fabric rectangle. Fuse, following manufacturer's directions. Peel off paper backing, and fuse main fabric rectangle to lining rectangle.

3. Fold bag in half, right sides together, and stitch center back seam. See diagram for Gift Bags, Step 5, on page 42.

4. Fold bag so center back seam is aligned with center front. Stitch across bottom of bag. See diagram for Step 6 on page 42.

5. For boxed bottom, refold one corner at bottom of bag to match diagram. See diagram for Step 7 on page 42. Measure 1¾″ from corner and draw a line perpendicular to seam. Stitch on line. Repeat at other corner. Turn bag right side out.

6. Press a ¼″ hem to outside of bag at top edge. Topstitch very close to cut edge. Press sides of bag following diagrams for Step 8 on page 42, measuring in 1¾″.

1.

2½″

·········· Cookie Bags ··········

Photo on page 61   Finished size 12½x5½x4″
Use 42-44″-wide fabric.

Yardage & Materials

Appliques – scraps	up to 5x7½″
Main fabric for bag	½ yd.
Lining	½ yd.
Paper-backed fusible web	⅝ yd.

Cutting Patterns on pages 50, 54

Applique pieces	use photo for colors
Main fabric	1 rectangle 15x19½″
Lining	1 rectangle 15x19½″
Fusible web	1 rectangle 15x19½″

Directions

Use ¼″ seam allowance unless otherwise noted.

1. Using your favorite method, applique one of the snowmen to the main fabric rectangle, centered from right to left and 2¾″ up from one of the 19½″ sides (bottom of bag).

2. Lay fusible web on wrong side of main fabric rectangle. Fuse, following manufacturer's directions. Peel off paper backing, and fuse main fabric rectangle to lining rectangle.

3. Fold bag in half, right sides together, and stitch center back seam. See diagram for Gift Bags, Step 5, on page 42.

4. Fold bag so center back seam is aligned with center front. Stitch across bottom of bag. See diagram for Step 6 on page 42.

5. For boxed bottom, refold one corner at bottom of bag to match diagram. See diagram for Step 7 on page 42. Measure 2″ from corner and draw a line perpendicular to seam. Stitch on line. Repeat at other corner. Turn bag right side out.

6. Press a ¼″ hem to inside of bag at top edge. Topstitch very close to cut edge. Press sides of bag following diagrams for Step 8 on page 42, measuring in 2″.

1.

2¾″

Sweatshirts

Photos on page 57
Snow Angel – patterns on pages 78
Poinsettia – patterns on page 76

Yardage & Materials

Purchased sweatshirt, prewashed & dried
Fabric scraps for applique   up to 7″ square

Directions

1. Cut applique pieces as desired using photos and diagrams as guides for color and placement.

2. Applique with your favorite method using photos and diagrams as guides for placement. Stem on poinsettia sweatshirt is fusible bias tape.

Hemmed Sweatshirts

Photos on page 57

Snowman & House – patterns on pages 51 & 54
Snowman & Marshmallows – patterns on p. 47-48
Santa – patterns on page 54 & 76

Yardage & Materials

Purchased sweatshirt, prewashed & dried
Fabric scraps for applique

Snow	5″ by width of sweatshirt
Marshmallow stick	2x12″
Others	up to 5x10″

Directions

1. Snowman Sweatshirts: Cut off bottom ribbing of sweatshirt. Cut a gentle curve on top of snow rectangle. Using your favorite method, applique snow to sweatshirt, bottom raw edge even with bottom raw edge of sweatshirt.

Santa Jacket: Cut off bottom ribbing and sleeve cuff ribbing. Lay flat on ironing board. Press body, making clear creases at each side. Fold in half, matching creases, and press center front line. Open out and check that pressed line is straight down center of sweatshirt. Cut on pressed line, cutting through neckline ribbing.

2. Snowman Sweatshirts: Press ½″ hem to right side of sweatshirt and buttonhole stitch in place by hand or machine.

Santa Jacket: Press ¾″ hems to **right** side of sweatshirt at center front and bottom of body and cuffs. *Open out. Turn bottom hem to **inside** of sweatshirt at center front, the opposite of the way it was pressed. Stitch along front fold line to encase raw edge. Turn hems to outside and poke corner out.* Press neckline ribbing to outside of sweatshirt so edge covers neckline seam. Repeat directions between stars at neckline edge. Buttonhole stitch all hems in place by hand or machine.

3. Cut applique pieces as desired using photos and diagrams as guides for color and placement.

4. Applique with your favorite method using photos and diagrams as guides for placement.

44

·······Pillow Patches······

Photo on page 28   Finished size 12″

Use 42-44″-wide fabric. When strips appear in the cutting list, cut crossgrain strips (selvage to selvage).

Yardage & Materials

Pillow cover	¾ yd.
Block background	⅓ yd.
Appliques	scraps up to 7x7″
Buttons	six ¾-⅞″
12″ pillow form	1

Cutting

Pillow cover	21½ x 26½″
Block background	8″ square
Applique pieces	Patterns on pages 68-69

Directions

Use ¼″ seam allowance unless otherwise noted.

1. Press 1½″ hem to wrong side of one 26½″ side of fabric rectangle. Press 1½″ to wrong side again, forming a hem of double thickness. Repeat on opposite side of rectangle. Do not stitch hems yet.

2. Fold pressed rectangle in half, wrong sides together, raw edges at bottom. Folded rectangle should now measure 15½x13¼″.

3. Center 8″ background square on pillow cover. Applique in place using your favorite method. Position and applique tree, Santa, or snowman.

4. Open out pillow cover, including pressed hems. Stitch 21½″ sides, right sides together. Press seam allowance to one side. Turn right side out.

5. Refold and pin pressed hems in place. Stitch each hem close to fold.

6. Make three buttonholes in top side of each hem, one at center and one spaced 3″ to either side. Stitch buttons under buttonholes.

7. Slide cover over pillow form and button up.

If you liked making these pillows, there are many more in our book, *Pillow Patches & Other Possibilities*. See page 80 for ordering information.

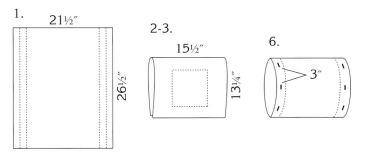

···········Mug Mats···········

Photo on page 61   Finished size 5″ square

Yardage For four

Flannel for front & back	8 scraps at least 6¼″ sq.
Appliques	scraps up to 4″ sq.
Batting scraps	8 scraps at least 6¼″ sq.
Potpourri (optional)	approx. 1 cup

Cutting For four

Flannel	4 squares 6¼″ for tops
	4 squares 5¾″ for backs
Applique pieces	Patterns on page 77
Batting	8 squares 6¼″

Directions

1. Applique one of the four designs, centered, on each of the 6¼″ flannel squares, using your favorite method.

2. Layer for each mat:
   a. two batting squares
   b. appliqued flannel square, right side up
   c. 5¾″ flannel square, right side down, centered on others

3. Stitch around 5¾″ square with a ⅜″ seam allowance, leaving 2½″ open on one side for turning. Trim large square even with small square. Trim corners. Turn through opening so batting is sandwiched between fabric layers. Press. Add ¼ cup potpourri between batting layers if desired. Stitch opening closed.

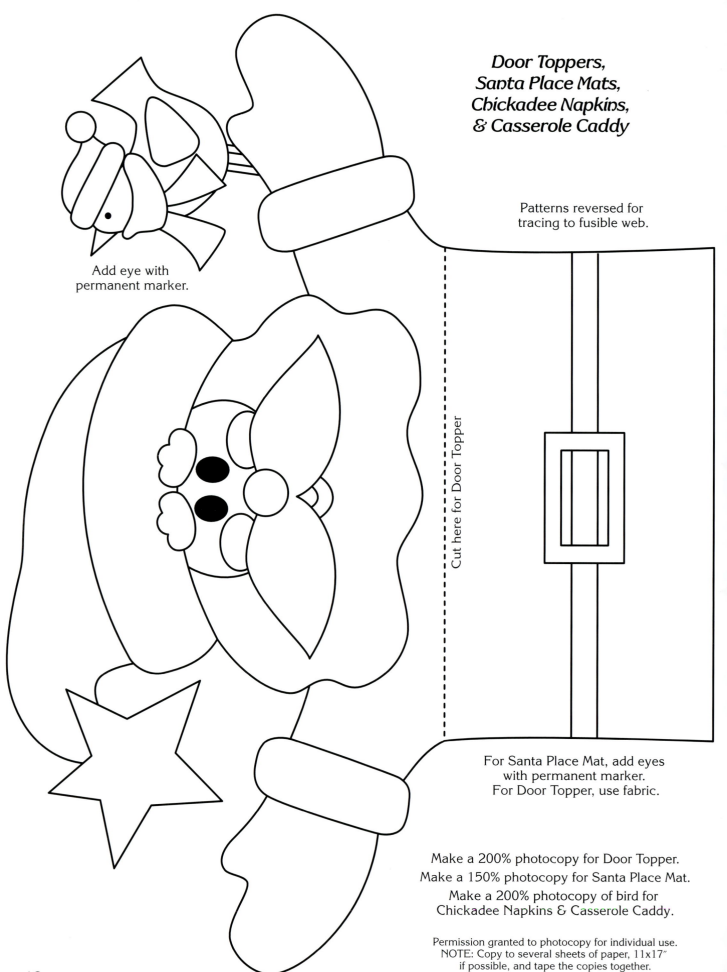

Door Toppers,
Santa Place Mats,
Chickadee Napkins,
& Casserole Caddy

Add eye with
permanent marker.

Patterns reversed for
tracing to fusible web.

Cut here for Door Topper

For Santa Place Mat, add eyes
with permanent marker.
For Door Topper, use fabric.

Make a 200% photocopy for Door Topper.
Make a 150% photocopy for Santa Place Mat.
Make a 200% photocopy of bird for
Chickadee Napkins & Casserole Caddy.

Permission granted to photocopy for individual use.
NOTE: Copy to several sheets of paper, 11x17″
if possible, and tape the copies together.

46

Add eyes & mouth
with permanent marker.

Patterns reversed for
tracing to fusible web.

Door Toppers

Add eyes & mouth
with permanent marker.

Hemmed Sweatshirts

Patterns reversed for
tracing to fusible web.

48

Snowflake Cookies

2 c. sugar
1 lb. margarine
2-3 tsp. vanilla
3 eggs
6 c. flour
1 tsp. baking powder
½ tsp. baking soda
1 tsp. salt

FROSTING
8 oz. softened cream cheese
1 stick margarine, softened
1 tsp. vanilla or almond extract
powdered sugar to make of
    spreading consistency

Blend well the sugar, margarine,
and vanilla. Add eggs one at a
time, mixing well after each
addition. Gradually add flour sifted
with baking powder, soda, and salt.
Mix well. Chill. Roll out to ¼"
thickness and cut with a snowflake
cookie cutter. Bake at 350° for 8-10
minutes. Cool on racks. Frost.

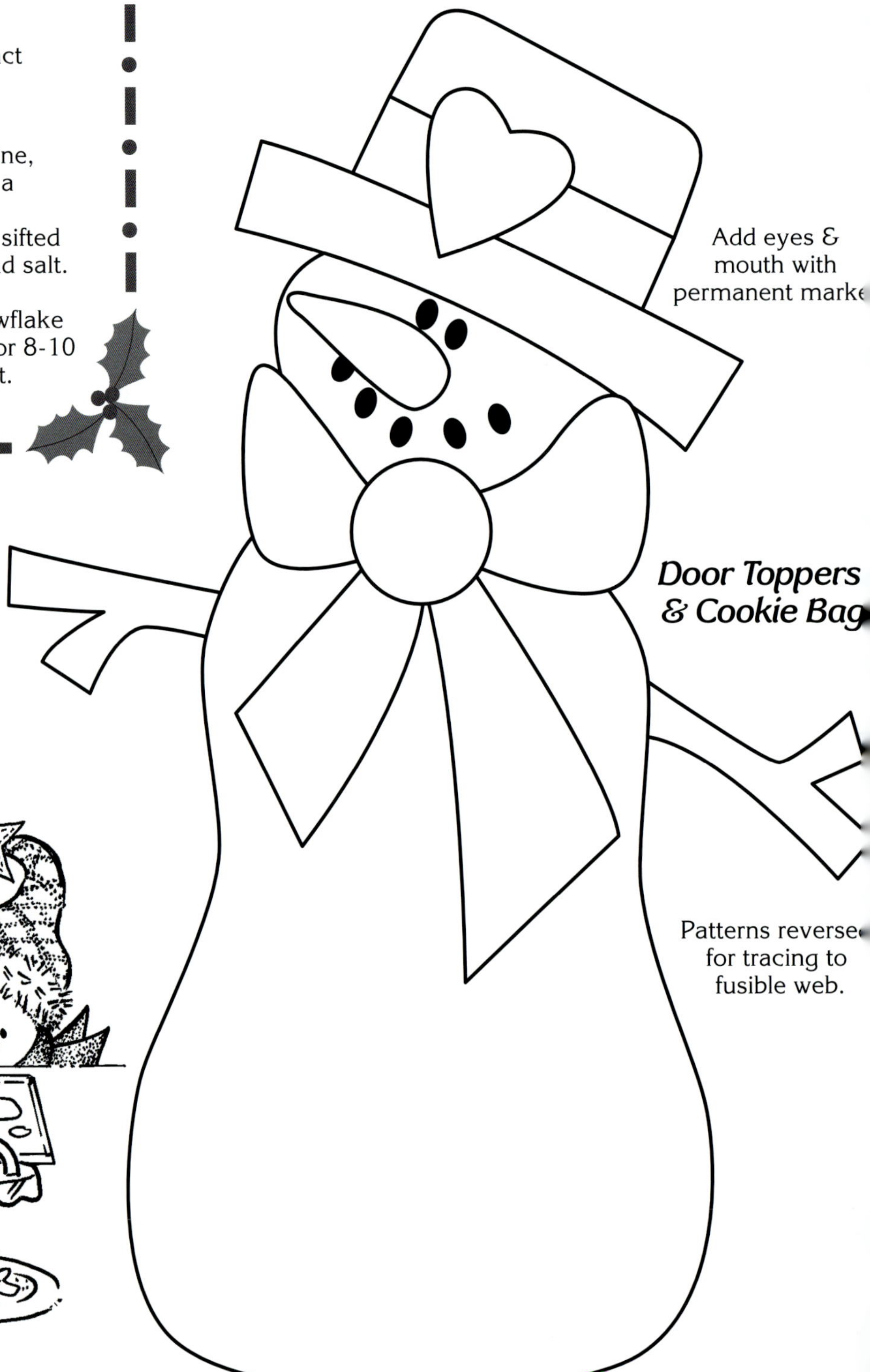

Add eyes &
mouth with
permanent marker

**Door Toppers
& Cookie Bag**

Patterns reverse
for tracing to
fusible web.

Door Toppers & Hemmed Sweatshirts

Chimney & Smoke

Add eyes & mouth
with permanent marker.

Patterns reversed for
tracing to fusible web.

Bear's Paw, Swags & Bows, & Carpenter's Wheel Tree Skirt   53

**Door Toppers,
Cookie Bags, &
Hemmed Sweatshirts**

Place on Fold

Make 200% photocopy of arch for full-sized pattern.

Permission granted to photocopy for individual use.
NOTE: Copy to several sheets of paper, 11x17"
if possible, and tape the copies together.

Cutting Line for Cardboard — — — Seamline

Background Arch

Also used for
Casserole
Caddy &
Chickadee
Napkins

Tree Trunks

Patterns reversed for
tracing to fusible web.

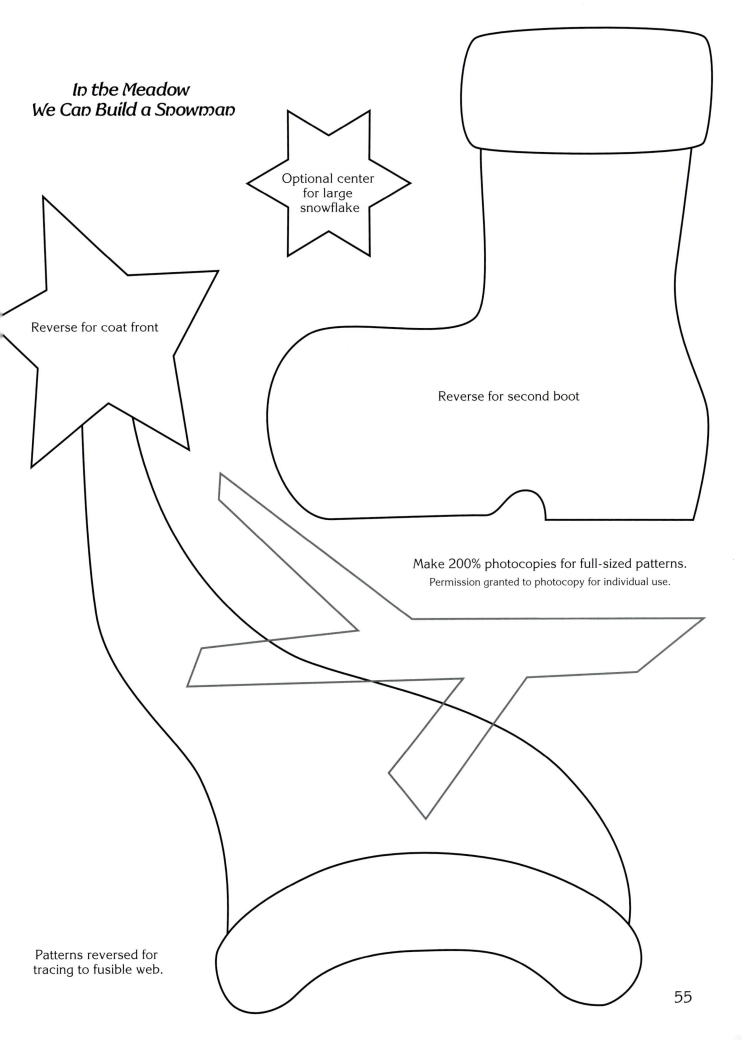

*In the Meadow
We Can Build a Snowman*

Optional center
for large
snowflake

Reverse for coat front

Reverse for second boot

Make 200% photocopies for full-sized patterns.
Permission granted to photocopy for individual use.

Patterns reversed for
tracing to fusible web.

In the Meadow
We Can Build a Snowman

Add eyes with
permanent marker.

Make 200% photocopies for full-sized patterns.

Permission granted to photocopy for individual use.
NOTE: Copy to several sheets of paper, 11x17″
if possible, and tape the copies together.

Patterns reversed for
tracing to fusible web.

Reverse for second mitten

In the Meadow
We Can Build a Snowman

Make 200% photocopies
for full-sized patterns.

Permission granted to
photocopy for individual use.

Patterns reversed for
tracing to fusible web.

59

60 Flannel Log Cabin, Log Cabin Pillow, Gathered Tree Skirt & Matching Ornaments
Photo index page 3

Christmas Card Holder, Aprons, Gift Bags, Wine Bags, Cookie Bags, Mug Mats, & Pull-a-Bow 61

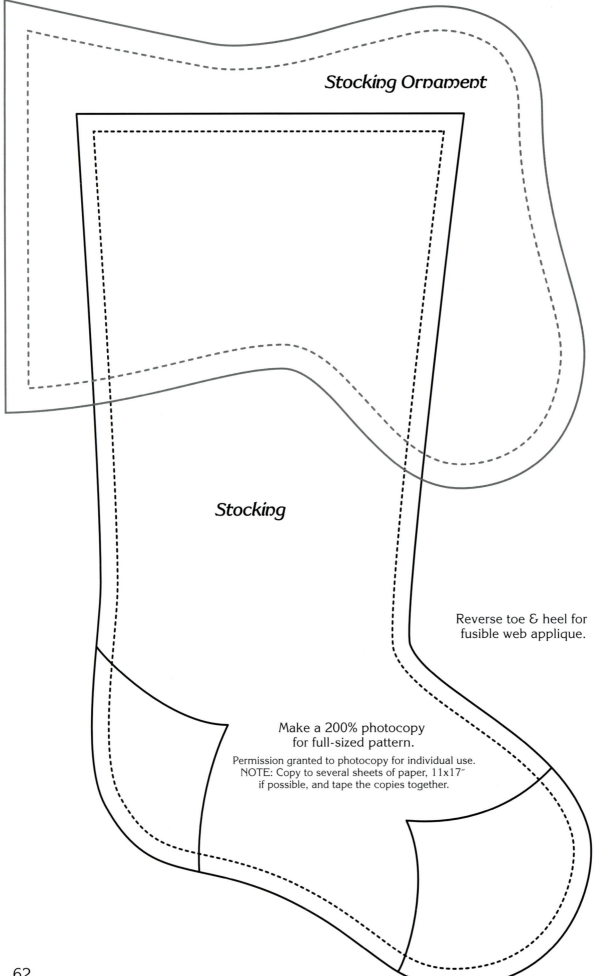

Stocking Ornament

Stocking

Reverse toe & heel for
fusible web applique.

Make a 200% photocopy
for full-sized pattern.

Permission granted to photocopy for individual use.
NOTE: Copy to several sheets of paper, 11x17″
if possible, and tape the copies together.

Let It Snow

Also used for In the Meadow We Can Build a Snowman

Also used for In the Meadow We Can Build a Snowman

Place dot on center & trace solid lines only.

63

64 Holly Berry Log Cabin
Photo index page 3

Use one or two
fabrics per leaf.

Holly Berry Log Cabin
& Holly Berry Tree Skirt

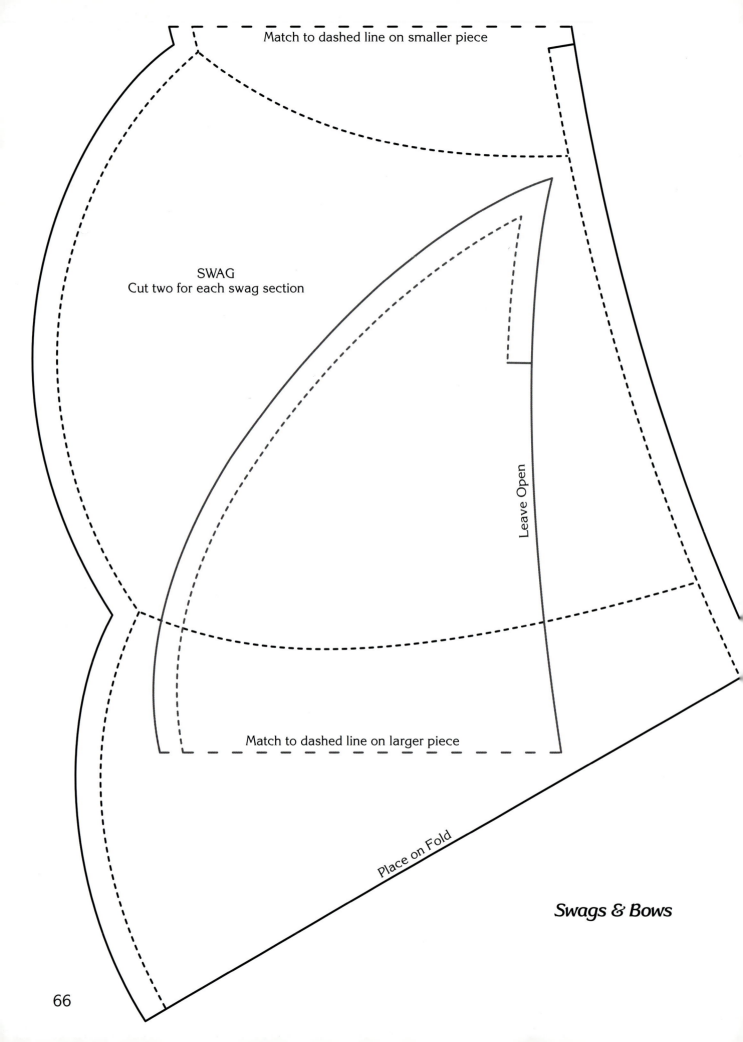

Match to dashed line on smaller piece

SWAG
Cut two for each swag section

Leave Open

Match to dashed line on larger piece

Place on Fold

Swags & Bows

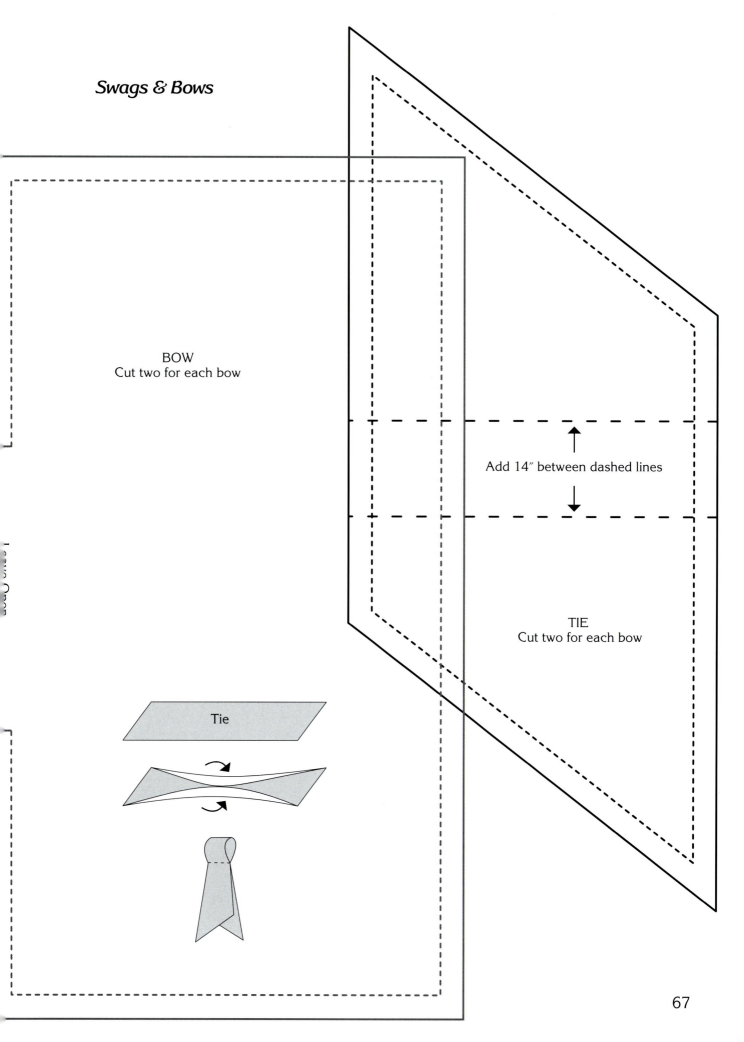

BOW
Cut two for each bow

Add 14″ between dashed lines

TIE
Cut two for each bow

Tie

Christmas Card Holder, Gift Bags, Pillow Patches, & Child's Snowman Apron

Paper Gift Bags & Place Cards

Use any of the applique patterns in this book, sized as needed, to make your own paper gift bags and place cards. Simply use favorite fabrics and fusible web applique.

Add eyes & mouth with permanent marker.

Make a 130% photocopy of snowman for child's apron. Use snowflakes & moon sized as given.

Make a 135% photocopy of snowman for Pillow Patches.

Permission granted to photocopy for individual use.

Patterns reversed for tracing to fusible web.

68

Add eyes with
permanent marker.

Patterns reversed for
tracing to fusible web.

Make 135% photocopies of
Santa & tree for Pillow Patches.

Permission granted to photocopy for individual use.

Child's Santa Apron

Add eyes with permanent marker.

Patterns reversed for tracing to fusible web.

Stars also used for Adult Tall Santa Apron

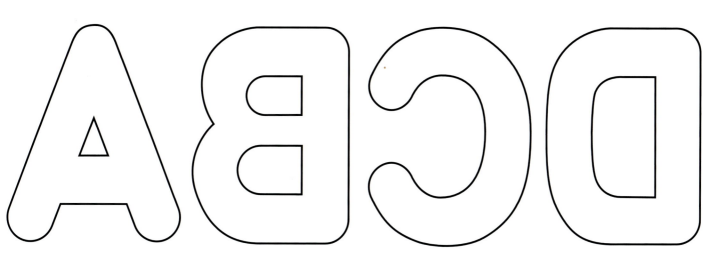

Christmas Card Holder, Santa Stockings,
& In the Meadow We Can Build a Snowman

Patterns reversed for
tracing to fusible web.

Noel Pillows

Make 200% photocopies
for full-sized patterns.

Permission granted to
photocopy for individual use.
NOTE: Copy to several
sheets of paper, 11x17″
if possible, and tape
the copies together.

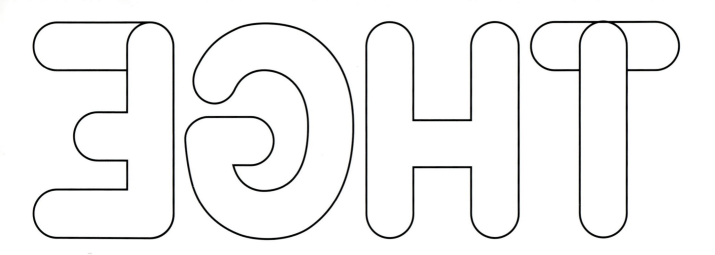

EIGHT

Christmas Card Holder, Santa Stockings,
& In the Meadow We Can Build a Snowman

Patterns reversed for
tracing to fusible web.

Noel Pillows

Make 200% photocopies
for full-sized patterns.

Permission granted to
photocopy for individual use.

Add face with
permanent marker.

Christmas Card Holder,
Santa Stockings, & In
the Meadow We Can
Build a Snowman

Noel Pillows

Make 200% photocopies
for full-sized patterns.

Permission granted to
photocopy for individual use.

Patterns reversed for
tracing to fusible web.

Add eyes & mouth
with permanent marker.

Christmas Card Holder,
Santa Stockings, &
In the Meadow We
Can Build a Snowman

Noel Pillows

Make 200% photocopies
for full-sized patterns.

Permission granted to
photocopy for individual use.

Patterns reversed for
tracing to fusible web.

Three Tall Santas, Wine Bags, Santa Stockings, & Adult Tall Santa Apron

Use one or two fabrics per leaf.

Add eyes with permanent marker.

Patterns reversed for tracing to fusible web.

Permission granted to photocopy for individual use.
NOTE: Copy to several sheets of paper, 11x17″
if possible, and tape the copies together.

Make 200% photocopies of Santas for full-sized Three Tall Santas quilt and Adult Tall Santa Apron patterns.
Make 120% photocopies of Santas for full-sized Santa Stocking patterns.

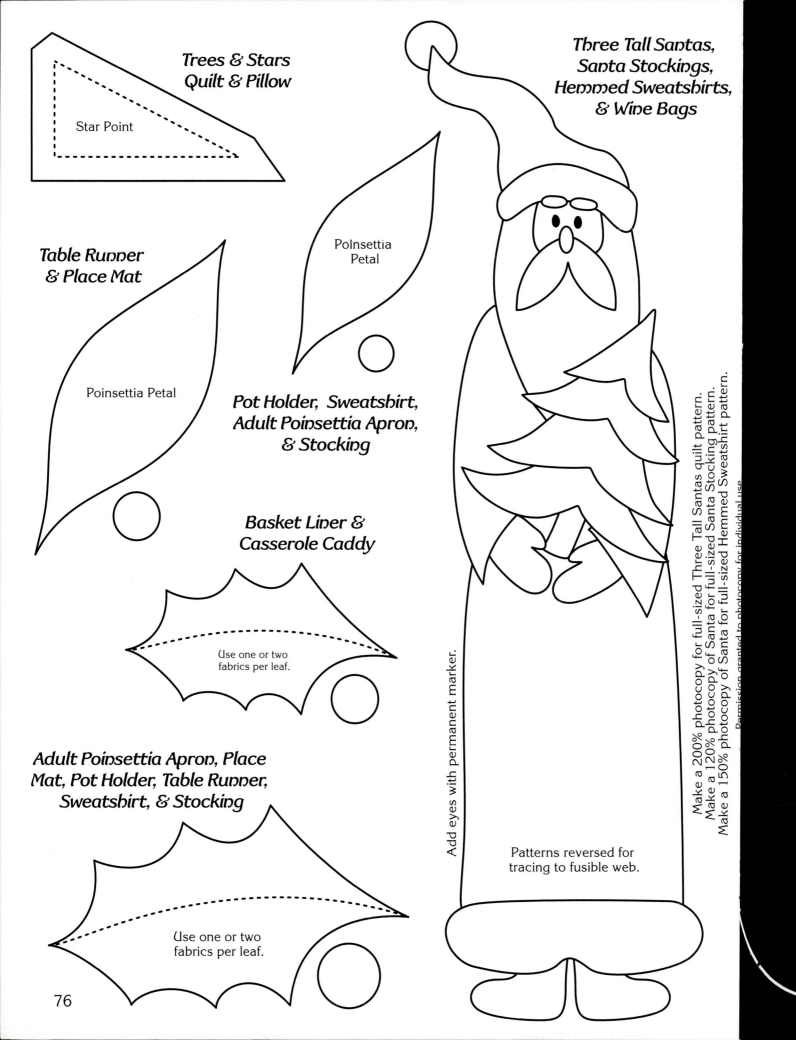

**Trees & Stars
Quilt & Pillow**

Star Point

**Three Tall Santas,
Santa Stockings,
Hemmed Sweatshirts,
& Wine Bags**

**Table Runner
& Place Mat**

Poinsettia
Petal

Poinsettia Petal

**Pot Holder, Sweatshirt,
Adult Poinsettia Apron,
& Stocking**

**Basket Liner &
Casserole Caddy**

Use one or two
fabrics per leaf.

**Adult Poinsettia Apron, Place
Mat, Pot Holder, Table Runner,
Sweatshirt, & Stocking**

Use one or two
fabrics per leaf.

Add eyes with permanent marker.

Patterns reversed for
tracing to fusible web.

Make a 200% photocopy for full-sized Three Tall Santas quilt pattern.
Make a 120% photocopy of Santa for full-sized Santa Stocking pattern.
Make a 150% photocopy of Santa for full-sized Hemmed Sweatshirt pattern.

Permission granted to photocopy for individual use.

Add eye with
permanent marker.

Patterns reversed for
tracing to fusible web.

In the Meadow We Can Build a Snowman

Snow Angel
Sweatshirt

Patterns reversed for
tracing to fusible web.

Add eyes & mouth
with permanent mark

78

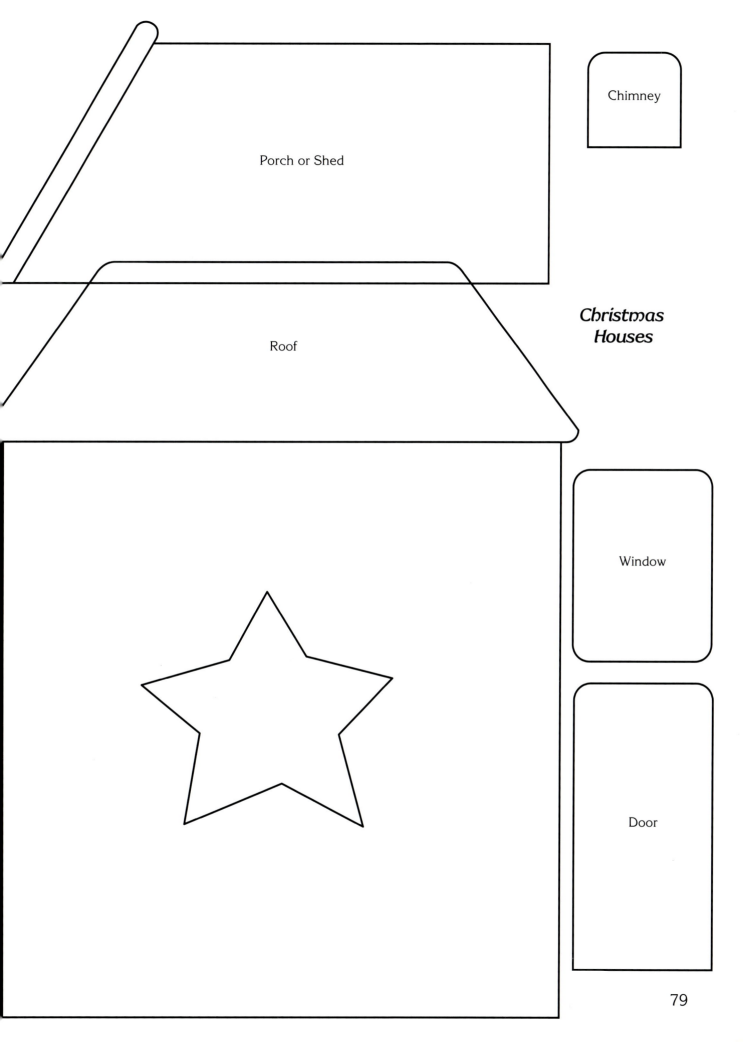

Porch or Shed

Chimney

Roof

Christmas Houses

Window

Door

Quilts For All Seasons from Possibilities®

Toppers

Toppers are beautiful quilts for displaying over bed pillows, on a bedspread or comforter, or on the back of a couch. Since you are only making half a quilt, it only takes half the time!

5 Easy Pieces

Make use of the beautiful large florals available now to make custom decorator-look quilts and accessories. Large blocks and applique shapes help speed you along.

HouseWarmers

Nineteen quilts and 25 project ideas for warming a home with the beauty of handmade quilts. Projects for every decor and skill level add personal touches to any room in the house.

Quilts & More

This informative book includes over 25 projects featuring photos transferred to fabric. Includes complete how-to instructions and full-sized patterns for making family heirlooms.

Album Coverups

Bring the creativity and fun of your memory book pages to the album cover. Use our ten great designs with easy fuse-and-use techniques to personalize your projects.

P.S. I Love You

One of the top 10 quilting books in America. Includes 17 quilts in cradle, crib, and twin sizes. Nursery accessories for making darling children's rooms. Exceptional collection!

P.S. I Love You Two

One of the new national top sellers–includes quilts in three sizes–little, crib, & twin. Timeless projects make cherished gifts. Complete directions and a multitude of techniques.

Pillow Patches

Making pillows has never been so easy or so much fun. Pillow covers can be changed at the flip of a button with the changes of season. Over 25 designs take you through the year.

Pillow Magic

Eight patchwork and applique blocks are made into pockets and attached to one pillow. Just turn them with the changing seasons! Extra block and directions for 9-block quilt.

Snow Buddies

Snow people so charming you won't want to save them just for winter! Monthly patterns perfect for decorating your home. Includes fusible applique directions.

Here Comes Santa Claus

A magical Santa with an engaging northwoods flavor. Buttonhole stitching enhances his sprightly step. Equally great for beginners as well as the more experienced.

POSSIBILITIES®

…Publishers of DreamSpinners® patterns, I'll Teach Myself® sewing products, and Possibilities® books…

Check with your local quilt shop. If not available, write or call us directly.

8970 East Hampden Avenue
Denver, Colorado 80231
303-740-6206 • Fax 303-220-7424
Orders only U.S. & Canada 1-800-474-2665
www.possibilitiesquilt.com

Home For Christmas

Dress up the Christmas tree with this simple-to-make tree skirt. A seasonal decoration that will be treasured for years to come! Directions for two variations. A great gift!